Inclusive Education for Autistic Children

of related interest

Concepts of Normality
The Autistic and Typical Spectrum
Wenn B. Lawson
ISBN 978 1 84310 604 3
eISBN 978 1 84642 829 6

It's Raining Cats and Dogs
An Autism Spectrum Guide to the Confusing World of
Idioms, Metaphors and Everyday Expressions
Michael Barton
ISBN 978 1 84905 283 2
eISBN 978 0 85700 588 5

Understanding and Evaluating Autism Theory
Nick Chown
ISBN 978 1 78592 050 9
eISBN 978 1 78450 306 2

The Neurodiverse Classroom
A Teacher's Guide to Individual Learning Needs and How to Meet Them
Victoria Honeybourne
ISBN 978 1 78592 362 3
eISBN 978 1 78450 703 9

Autism and Flexischooling
A Shared Classroom and Homeschooling Approach
Clare Lawrence
ISBN 978 1 84905 279 5
eISBN 978 0 85700 582 3

Forest School and Autism
A Practical Guide
Michael James
ISBN 978 178592 291 6
eISBN 978 1 78450 595 0

Inclusive Education
for
Autistic Children

Helping Children and Young People to
Learn and Flourish in the Classroom

Dr Rebecca Wood

Foreword by Dr Wenn B. Lawson
Illustrated by Sonny Hallett

Jessica Kingsley *Publishers*
London and Philadelphia

First published in 2019
by Jessica Kingsley Publishers
73 Collier Street
London N1 9BE, UK
and
400 Market Street, Suite 400
Philadelphia, PA 19106, USA

www.jkp.com

Library of Congress Cataloging in Publication Data
Names: Wood, Rebecca author.
Title: Inclusive education for autistic children : helping children and young
    people to learn and flourish in the classroom / Dr Rebecca Wood.
Description: Philadelphia : Jessica Kingsley Publishers, 2019.
Identifiers: LCCN 2019008230 | ISBN 9781785923210
Subjects: LCSH: Autistic children--Education--Great Britain. | Inclusive
    education--Great Britain.
Classification: LCC LC4719.G78 W66 2019 | DDC 371.94--
dc23 LC record available at https://catalog.loc.gov/vwebv/
search?searchCode=LCCN&searchArg=2019008230&searchType=1&permalink=y

British Library Cataloguing in Publication Data
A CIP catalogue record for this book is available from the British Library

ISBN 978 1 78592 321 0
eISBN 978 1 78450 634 6

Printed and bound in Great Britain

For Wanda:

I meant what I said on that day

Contents

Foreword

DR WENN B. LAWSON

As an older autistic, although still learning, I live at the other end of life's schooling. Life always has so much to teach us, but traditional beliefs in Western Society in how we educate children have dictated that inclusion means including all, but not necessarily in the ways they need. Rebecca's book invites readers to consider the different meanings of inclusion and how it might be achieved.

A key component of this process is to listen to, observe and engage with autistic children and adults. This book, based on research involving 20 autistic people, and incorporating the views and perspectives of a further eight autistic contributors whose comments are woven throughout all of the chapters, puts the views of autistic children and adults at the centre of arguments about how to improve their educational inclusion, well-being and longer-term outcomes. These discussions are further illuminated with illustrations from the autistic artist Sonny Hallett, as well as research findings involving school staff and the parents of autistic children.

When children fail to learn, all too often we blame the child. Our focus on 'what's wrong' or 'what's the problem?' needs to change. As Rebecca rightly argues, by appreciating the aptitudes, characteristics and learning styles of autistic children, we not only facilitate their inclusion, but also make school life easier and more enjoyable for everyone. We must move away from seeing autism as 'a problem' and instead, move to welcome the autistic individual with their unique strengths and abilities. Instead of looking at what we do wrong, we must explore what it is we do right. This way, when we use what works, we can apply this to areas that have posed problems in the past.

For autistic individuals, and as discussed in Chapters 2 and 3, inclusion is thought to imply the necessary provision of a sensory environment that considers sensory needs (they vary from child to child). Providing a classroom environment that is calm, structured, uses natural lighting as far as possible (no fluorescent lights, as they are a trigger for epilepsy) and making arrangements for more flexible teaching that considers the needs of the whole child are vital to any successful outcome. Therefore, inclusion also means adapting to the learning styles of autistic children, understanding how they respond to different aspects of the curriculum and thinking carefully about their educational priorities, as discussed in Chapters 4, 5 and 6. It's also about the support they receive, which is considered in Chapter 7, as well as understanding how they communicate and prefer to socialise, which are explored in Chapters 8 and 9.

Being single-minded and able to focus on one thing at any one time, once interest is sparked, is a useful tool in the classroom. The importance of facilitating individual interest cannot be understated and this is discussed frequently in this book, but especially in Chapter 5. It's easy to think if we are only interested in certain areas, topics or subjects, this is a hindrance to exploring the bigger picture. However, research shown throughout this book depicts another story. It demonstrates (as does my own research) that interest, thought of as 'passion' and not 'obsession', can be the means to accessing the bigger picture. If school and family alike will take the time to invest in who we are as autistic people, the rewards will outweigh the obstacles.

For autistic individuals, appreciating object permanence (that objects have a life of their own, even when out of sight) can also apply to people, events and emotions. So, understanding all these elements needs to be built into the art of inclusion to make school and learning accessible. For example, how do I cope with 'change' if I have difficulties forward thinking? How can I enjoy and play a game, like 'Hide Go Seek' if I believe once I can't see you, you are gone forever?

The difficulty is that very few schools are equipped to meet these needs, either with school layout and equipment, as echoed in Chapter 2, or with the necessary trained staff, as discussed in Chapter 7. Therefore, 'inclusion' – having a child present but without the necessary adaptations to truly include them – highlights the child's inability and exaggerates their sense of isolation. This means, rather than fostering a sense of belonging, it causes children to feel excluded, as argued in Chapter 3.

As a younger person I 'lived' in my baseball cap. My cap served to slightly limit my field of vision to help prevent sensory overwhelm, gave pressure to my head so I knew where I ended and helped me navigate open space. If I was made to remove my cap, my attention went with it and I became inattentive in class. Some sensory sensibilities are easily accommodated (the wearing of ear defenders, needing to work on soft or hard surfaces, going into a room first, rather than last, wearing a 'squeeze jacket' or avoiding smelly perfumes) while other sensory differences are not so well understood. For example, I'm a synesthetic and I experience colours as indicators of emotions rather than only feeling them. I certainly am a feeling person and have many different 'feelings', but they are possibly a bit vague and blurred around the edges. This is another reason why it's important to get to know us individually, as it's not one size fits all.

In addition, although we must consider sensory sensibilities, if we employ universal design – as discussed at different points throughout the book – we will be catering for autistic children and the whole school community. Beginning in the way we mean to go is much wiser than having to chart a new course when we discover the one we are on is not taking us where we need to go. However, it is better to adapt what we have rather than abandon ship.

Autism has traditionally been thought of as a more 'male' disposition that occurs much less in females. We now know this is not the case. But females presenting with the same difficulties, via their female personhood, will demonstrate differing behaviours than boys and may learn to 'mask' their difficulties. Rebecca briefly discusses some of these issues in the first and final chapters of her book, and concludes with some thought-provoking suggestions of what the future might hold, both in terms of education practice and ongoing research.

This important guide to true inclusion, which is based on several years' research as well as Rebecca's practical experience in the education sector, opens our eyes to enable both teachers and families to explore ways to include, incorporate and incite cooperative relationships that foster inclusive practice. Using autistic strengths and interests to build bridges across the areas outlined above, and echoed within this text, are vital to creating true inclusion at school.

Acknowledgements

I would like to thank the participants in my original research study: the school staff who gave me their time and tolerated my intrusion into their workplaces, and especially the SENCOs, who were the lynchpin to my data collection in schools. As a parent of an autistic child myself whose time is often taken up with 'the business of SEND', I also appreciate the fact that the parents took the trouble to talk to me, and to share their ideas, fears and hopes for the future of their children. The 10 autistic adults in my study were also generous with their time and the thoughts they offered, which were of vital importance in my research. However, my main focus was on the autistic children in the schools where my research took place, and they were all friendly, cooperative and honest: I hope they go on to have the fulfilling and happy futures they deserve. In addition, I am grateful for the funding by way of a scholarship I received from the University of Birmingham, which enabled me to complete a PhD without experiencing financial hardship. Thanks are also due to my supervisors Professor Karen Guldberg and Dr Kerstin Wittemeyer.

Particular thanks are owed to the 10 contributors to this book, as well as the parents of the children and young people who helped with this process. Their input provides an essential authenticity to the different chapters. I'm also grateful to Jessica Kingsley Publishers, for being brave enough to commission a book about autism education that doesn't contain any strategies or techniques, and for being flexible around submission dates too. In addition, if I hadn't received funding by way of a postdoctoral fellowship at King's College London from the Economic and Social Research Council, it would have been very difficult to complete this book.

Also deserving of thanks are those who have either helped directly with suggestions and comments or have simply provided background encouragement as I navigate the choppy waters of academe: Professor Francesca Happé, David Jackson-Perry, Ruth Moyse, Catherine Older, Professor Katherine Runswick-Cole, Dr Catriona Stewart and Professor Gary Thomas. I'd like to thank my contributors Michael Barton, Kabie Brook, Sonny Hallett and George Whitney, for their very helpful chapter reviews, and I will also mention here the autistic researcher Michelle Dawson, who I do not know personally, but who contributes a great deal to the autism research field in a number of ways. And, of course, there is my loving husband Dr Alan McIntosh and my intelligent and sensitive son, who continues to remind me of what really matters. If there is a central message in this book, it is to put the perspectives of autistic children at the heart of things in autism education practice and research.

The Contributors

'Grace'

Grace is 14 years old and loves to draw. She adores her cats and has many friends at school but only a few best friends and spends lots of time with them. Grace enjoys ICT and art at school but doesn't really like the other subjects very much. She likes watching anime and reading manga, and *Attack on Titan* is her favourite. She is an animal lover and is very passionate about the conservation of wildlife, particularly big cats, and hopes to help protect them by donating to charities. Grace is quiet and shy but thinks she's a good friend.

'James'

James is 8 years old and lives with his mum, dad, older brother and two dogs. He loves Wikipedia and learning facts about everything so he can tell people them. His favourite pastime is history: at the moment this is movie history of the 1930s and 1940s. James finds it hard to tell people how he is feeling, and this makes him anxious. But his friends say he is always the first to help if they are sad or hurt, and he is great to be around, especially when he is excited about something. James is very proud of himself.

'Rose'

Rose is 8 years old. She has long, blonde hair and likes to play with her friends. Rose is exciting and funny and loves going wild with her friends. She is clever and smart and does her work whenever she is asked to. Rose only likes a few foods. She likes YouTube, Roblox, Minecraft and Glitter Force on Netflix. Rose enjoys Christmas because of the presents, Halloween because she likes dressing up as a scary person, and Easter because finding the eggs is like a treasure hunt.

'Zack'

Zack is 10 years old and lives with his mum, dad and three siblings. He loves making breakfast for his youngest sister. Zack really enjoys playing on his Xbox: his favourite games are WWE 2K17, Sunset Overdrive and Overdrive by Titan. He really likes going to the park to play on the gym equipment, going out with his mum and borrowing audiobooks from the library to listen to at home. Zack's favourite foods are pepperoni pizza, cheese toasties and macaroni cheese. As a treat, he sometimes goes out with his mum for a cheese toastie. Zack doesn't really like school – he finds it hard.

Jon Adams

Jon Adams is an autistic artist who works cross-platform in image, word, sound, performance and public art, weaving in fragments of autobiography, science and hidden metaphor. The result is a unique visual perspective of recording and systemising history, time and place. He has worked with London 2012, the Imperial War Museum, Professor Simon Baron-Cohen and Sir Peter Brook. He actively feeds into national arts policy and debate around the abilities of artists, diversity and digital inclusivity, and is campaigning for parity in the arts for neurodivergent artists through Flow Observatorium.

Michael Barton

Michael Barton is the author of *It's Raining Cats and Dogs* and *A Different Kettle of Fish*, both published by Jessica Kingsley Publishers. He works as a data analyst and is patron of CASPA, a charity based in South East London. Michael is an experienced speaker on autism and Asperger's syndrome, having spoken since he was 18 alongside world-renowned speakers. He gives talks at a wide variety of events across the UK, focusing on the positive aspects of being autistic. In his spare time, he is an accomplished musician, a black belt in judo and a keen rock climber.

Kabie Brook

Kabie Brook is an autistic activist and campaigner, co-founder and current chair of ARGH (Autism Rights Group Highland), and has 30 years' experience working with and for Autistic people of all ages. Kabie is a member of the National Autism Strategy Governance Group (Scotland), has helped develop training materials for the National Autistic Society (NAS), is a community advisor for Police Scotland and collaborated on the newly launched Autistic Space Kit (ASK) App. In 2016 Kabie organised and led the first Autistic Europe Fringe and is committed to creating useful autistic-led spaces and the promotion of autistic-led initiatives.

Sonny Hallett

Sonny Hallett is an artist, writer and autistic activist based in Edinburgh. They are a co-founder and chair of the Autistic Mutual Aid Society Edinburgh (AMASE), and have a keen interest in promoting the autistic community and in participatory research in autism, especially autism and mental health. Their illustration work ranges from science communication to comics and children's book illustration.

Dr Wenn B. Lawson

Dr Lawson, autistic lecturer, psychologist, researcher, advocate, writer and poet, has passionately shared his professional and personal knowledge about autism for 25 years. He has written and/or contributed to over 20 books and many papers. He is a tutor for the University of Birmingham's Master's in Autism course, a participant at the Autism Cooperative Research Centre (Autism CRC), Australia, a member of the 'I CAN' board, Australia, and resides on the editorial board for the journal *Autism in Adulthood*. Dr Lawson also consults for the South Australian Government. He is a family man with autistic and non-autistic children and grandchildren. In 2017 he presented to the United Nations on autism and ageing.

George Whitney

George Whitney lives with his family and his many pets and is studying IT at college. He enjoys playing video games, building LEGO®, watching TV, going to the cinema and spending time with his friends. George has been a student rep at school and college for many years. He is passionate about representing students' views and ensuring people with disabilities have the correct support. George has given talks to staff at college about being on the autism spectrum. He is also a co-chair on the steering group for a local charity that supports the families of children and young people with disabilities.

Introduction

When I started my PhD, on which this book is based, in 2013, I wasn't sure at that point what exactly I wanted to research. Autism – for sure. Education – definitely. Exclusion – absolutely. Because the sad fact is, autistic children experience high levels of exclusion *from* school, a pattern that starts in the early years, and continues onwards, right through to adult education and lifelong learning. And as the learned Professor Gary Thomas put it, when writing more generally about children with special educational needs and disabilities (SEND), it's not just about the simple fact of being on the wrong side of the school gates, but concerns 'the damage done to individuals' sense of worth and identity' when some children realise they are 'conspicuously excluded from the expectations, the activities, the resources, the worlds' of their peers (Thomas 2012, p.480). In simple terms, to be excluded from school is to be excluded from society, or at least, to be much more likely to be so, in the longer term.

What I found in the five schools where my data collection took place, and describe in the different chapters of this book, is that inclusion doesn't just mean being physically present in school, and that autistic children experience many mini-exclusions in the form of part-time timetables, alternative targets and being segregated from their peers. At the same time, however, I was determined that my PhD was going to be constructive. I didn't want to just wallow in the problems, but to seek solutions to them. And I discovered that while exclusion can be multi-faceted, inclusion can be too, and that school staff, autistic children and their parents often work creatively and flexibly to make it work. So while this book certainly does not stint on delineating the problems experienced by autistic children in schools, it also offers, I hope, plenty of ideas and insights that show how the status quo could be improved.

Central to my research were my participants, consisting of 36 school staff (teaching assistants, teachers, special educational needs coordinators (SENCOs), deputy head teachers), 10 autistic children, 10 parents and 10 autistic adults. Apart from the autistic adults, who were scattered across the UK, my participants were based in five mainstream schools in England. Bringing together and analysing their different perspectives in a case study was an important component of my approach, because 1 felt strongly that if 1 just talked to teachers, for example, or only interviewed parents, 1 would get quite a patchy idea of the situation. And if having these different viewpoints within my study was important, understanding the perspectives and experiences of autistic children and adults in particular was essential. Time and again 1 found that issues aired say, by teachers, would be completely reframed when the autistic adults discussed the same points. Or the experiences of the autistic children would give vital clues as to how they should be supported and encouraged to learn, as well as to be themselves and develop their own personalities, attributes and interests.

1 have continued this drive to prioritise autistic viewpoints and perspectives in this book in which 1 share and discuss my PhD findings. You will see that 1 have recruited a number of new autistic contributors to help with this process. The comments from four autistic children – Grace, James, Rose and Zack (not their real names) – and four autistic adults – Jon Adams, Michael Barton, Kabie Brook and George Whitney – are woven throughout each of the chapters. All of their comments are drawn from questionnaires that they either completed independently, or with help from me and/or a parent. You will see that some of the contributors are much more loquacious than others, and that 1 have respected their individual approaches in the book. As a result, some have a lot more to say than others, and on occasions they don't all share the same opinions, but all provide vital insights into the topics discussed throughout the book. In addition, the chapters are illuminated with illustrations from the talented autistic artist Sonny Hallett, Jon Adams has also provided a drawing to elucidate one of his anecdotes, and the Foreword is written by the autistic writer and academic Dr Wenn B. Lawson. For me, Wenn is something of a pioneer, and his book *Concepts of Normality* (2008), which 1 read at an early stage of my research, changed the whole direction of

my PhD. As a parent of an autistic child myself, I am relieved that someone like Wenn is out there, writing and speaking about autism in his gentle and perceptive way.

Back in 2013, there were few studies that involved autistic children and adults as active participants in autism research. Instead they were very often simply objects of study, and the aim was to find out what was wrong with them rather than to understand their perspectives. Even in 2016, when I first drafted the proposal of this book, making it clear that there would be a number of autistic contributors, it was a fairly uncommon approach. I'm glad to see, however, that this idea is gaining traction more widely, and, of course, that increasingly, autistic people are not simply 'featuring' in someone else's research, but leading their own research projects and other schemes. As you can see from the information about the contributors preceding this Introduction, I was very fortunate to secure their involvement in this book.

I hope that teachers and other education staff, trainee teachers and students on undergraduate, postgraduate autism and SEND courses, SENCOs, autism practitioners, associated professionals such as speech and language therapists and educational psychologists, parents and early career researchers will see the benefits of a practical book strongly informed by original research which puts autistic children and adults at the heart of things. What I hope it shows is that rather than applying strategies and interventions, it is only by engaging with autistic children and young people as unique individuals, appreciating their skills and aptitudes, their ways of communicating and social preferences, that much more positive outcomes are likely to arise. And not just for them, but also for their peers, and the teachers who teach them.

Of course, autistic children may well need help in some ways, just as other children do, but the key is to try to understand and connect with them, not change them from who they are. And as a former teacher and autism practitioner myself, I do have some idea of the practical difficulties faced by school staff. When all is said and done, schools were not designed with autistic children in mind, and even the most perceptive, inclusive and caring staff will struggle to achieve the flexibility autistic children and others need within the current set-up. Inclusion will only work when it is planned for from the get-go, rather than an add-on after the fact.

In my book, I have covered a number of areas that relate to the educational inclusion of autistic children. You will see that while all of the chapters are informed by research, some are more practice-oriented than others. And as a general textbook, rather than focusing only on a single topic such as communication, for example, I necessarily have not been able to go into depth in all of the aspects covered. In addition, I have limited this analysis to my research findings and only occasionally stray beyond this. In other words, I try not to write about issues I have no empirical data to support, and therefore only touch briefly on issues such as gender and neurodiversity, for example. In addition, some points apply to younger, primary schoolchildren only, as my data collection took place in primary schools. Nevertheless, I have not limited myself to this age group, and also include discussions relevant to older autistic young people and adults.

Chapter 1

Descriptions of Autism

Introduction

You might think, given the amount of discussion in the media, the plentiful research, the training programmes, government and charity initiatives, projects and laws, that we are all operating on a shared understanding of what autism *is*. But whether you are autistic yourself, work with autistic children and adults, conduct research into autism, are a relative of an autistic person, or indeed, a combination of some or all of these, I'm pretty sure that you would find the question – What is autism? – quite difficult to answer. And that even if you did manage to come up with a response, it's very likely that your answer would differ from that of many other people, just as theirs would differ from yours and everyone else's. When you think about it, this is a somewhat startling state of affairs, given the huge amount of effort and attention that is currently directed at this phenomenon called 'autism'. Not only this, but we have to wonder about the impact this uncertainty might be having on autistic children in schools, as different people, with different conceptualisations of autism, interact with and respond to the children in different ways.

Interestingly, many of the 50 or so adults in my own study struggled to define or describe autism, even though they all had a major connection with it, to the extent that they either taught autistic children, or were the parents of an autistic child, or indeed, were autistic themselves. Even some of the autistic adults were uncertain how to respond, and when they did so, their answers varied between them. In fact, defining autism *is* very difficult, for reasons that will be explored more fully throughout the book. So if you're thinking the same as my research participants – that you can't really say what autism is – that is, in my view, a good sign, and a helpful mindset to have as you make your way through the different chapters of this book.

In this chapter, I'm going to try to unpick some of these varied understandings of autism and suggest how this confusion might have arisen. I consider issues of autism prevalence and diagnosis, and explore briefly the supposed 'causes' of autism and the impact this has on research priorities, as well as the ensuing interventions. I also discuss the usefulness – or not – of describing autism as 'a form of difference', and the associated problem of 'othering': what this is and how it might arise. I touch on the concept of neurodiversity, discuss whether or not autism should be considered to be a disability, and consider briefly questions about gender. And at the end of this chapter, because it is closely linked to the issues discussed, I explain my use of autism terminology in the book.

How many people are autistic?

I'm tempted to write, in response to this question: *I don't know.* But before you throw this book away on the assumption that I don't have a clue what I'm talking about, please do read on, because I have very good reasons for asserting that no one actually knows how many people are autistic, and if they say they do, then they are, in some senses anyway, *wrong.* Let me explain.

As far as the research is concerned, the prevalence figures for autism vary a great deal. Baird *et al.* (2006), for example, based on a large study in the South Thames area of the UK, found an autism prevalence of 1.16 per cent. The Office for National Statistics (ONS) reflected this in 2011, recording a rate of 1.1 per cent amongst children aged 4 to 16. In a relatively small study based in Cambridgeshire, Baron-Cohen *et al.* (2009b) found a rate of 1.54 per cent of children aged 5 to 9, and Brugha *et al.* (2011) considered that just under 1 per cent of adults are autistic. So these are all *more or less* similar. However, using the UK-wide Millennium Cohort Study, which included data from 18,522 families, Dillenburger *et al.* (2015) found that 3.5 per cent of children are diagnosed with autism by the time they are 11 years of age, a far greater number than most previous studies have shown.

The figures vary even more if we consider research beyond the UK. Y.S. Kim *et al.* (2011), for example, in a study based in a South Korean community, found a rate of 2.64 per cent amongst children between the ages of 7 and 12. In the USA, Christensen *et al.* (2016) found a rate of 1 in 68 children, followed by Baio *et al.* (2018), with a rate of 1 in 59: these are all figures significantly in excess of previous ones. Indeed, amongst other issues, these variations in prevalence figures also point to the fact that understandings of autism are at least in part culturally determined, a phenomenon described by Papadopoulos (2016) in a study comparing the attitudes of

UK-based Nigerian and English people towards a diagnosis of autism. Similarly, H. Kim (2012), in a very small, but nevertheless fascinating, study considering how autism is conceptualised in Canada, Nicaragua and Korea, found that how people identified and responded to autism varied according to societal norms. Indeed, some commentators even argue that 'autism' as a concept and as a diagnosis should be set aside altogether (Runswick-Cole, Mallett and Timimi 2016).

> People are never one thing. I have ADHD/Tourette's and autism, for example. There's a lot of autisms in a way, there's a lot of things people group under one banner. (Jon)

How is an autism diagnosis made?

Most diagnoses of autism are achieved through medical assessments, be they via paediatricians in the case of children, or psychologists and psychiatrists for adults. In the UK, and especially for children, these processes might be facilitated by a 'multi-disciplinary team' approach, and so can be substantiated by quasi-medical assessments in the form of speech and language or occupational therapy reports, for example. They may also involve staff from an educational setting or information from parents, although these can be viewed as second-order inputs, of inferior value to medical wisdom and know-how (see Hodge and Runswick-Cole (2008) on how parental input can be devalued). And so we must ask, do certain medical practitioners therefore 'know' what autism is, and if so, how did they come to acquire this knowledge?

When conducting an assessment for autism, medical practitioners often use specific diagnostic tools such as the Autism Diagnostic Observation Schedule (ADOS), the Autism Diagnosis Interview-Revised (ADI-R), the Childhood Autism Rating Scale (CARS) or the Diagnostic Instrument for Social and Communication Disorders (DISCO), although there are a number of others. These tools are themselves derived from weighty diagnostic manuals, considered to be the benchmark for the identification and description of medical conditions, with the *Diagnostic and Statistical Manual of Mental Disorders* (DSM) and the *International Classification of Diseases* (ICD) constituting the principal publications in this area.

These are updated every few years or so, leading to revisions of the diagnostic tools too.

So let's take a moment – still bearing in mind that many of us find it difficult to define autism – to consider how autism is described in these powerful and influential medical tomes. According to the DSM-5 (APA 2013), for example, autism consists of 'persistent deficits in social communication and social interaction across multiple contexts', which might be manifested by 'deficits in social-emotional reciprocity' and an 'abnormal social approach'. In addition, it is stated that the 'severity' of the autism depends on the extent to which a person demonstrates 'restricted, repetitive patterns of behavior, interests, or activities', which could be evidenced by an 'insistence on sameness, inflexible adherence to routines', as well as an 'unusual interest in sensory aspects of the environment'.[1] Meanwhile, the ICD-11 (WHO 2018) refers to 'persistent deficits in the ability to initiate and to sustain reciprocal social interaction and social communication', as well as 'a range of restricted, repetitive, and inflexible patterns of behaviour and interests' as being indicative of autism, as long as they constitute impairment.[2] Even though I don't have space here to include the full descriptions – which continue along the same lines in any case – with words such as 'deficits' and 'disorder', it doesn't seem from these accounts that being diagnosed with autism is in any way desirable. According to these prominent medical definitions, autism is a highly problematic condition, a diagnosis we should fear, either for ourselves or our loved ones, or the children we teach.

Setting aside the question of how 'abnormal' or 'unusual' such characteristics are if at least 1 in 100 people possess them, we must consider the widespread impact of such negative descriptions, where autism is characterised by profound deficits in communication, social interaction, behaviour and functioning. Even though these traits and attributes are considered to vary in 'severity', this 'medical model', where autism is classified along with diseases and illnesses, arguably constitutes the bedrock to understandings of autism internationally, permeating the several layers of medical, administrative, educational and societal

---

1   See www.cdc.gov/ncbddd/autism/hcp-dsm.html
2   See https://icd.who.int/browse11/l-m/en

structures and organisations. Moreover, such descriptions have barely – if at all – moved on from the pivotal notion of the 'triad of impairments' as defined by Wing (1980), whereby autism was considered to consist of 'severe impairments of social interaction, language abnormalities, and repetitive stereotyped behaviors' (Wing and Gould 1979, p.11). This is despite the fact that this highly reputed and pioneering study did not include any children in mainstream schools or resource provisions (Cigman 2007; Gould 2017), suggesting a significant limitation in sampling that is rarely taken into consideration. Nevertheless, even though, as we shall see, alternative – and perhaps more compelling – descriptions of autism exist, those derived from the DSM and ICD do appear clear and unequivocal. So why did my research participants – all of whom had knowledge and experience of autism diagnosis to a greater or lesser extent – find describing autism so difficult?

Well, many of the non-autistic adults in particular appeared highly aware of the deficit-oriented medical descriptions outlined earlier, with several referring to communication difficulties and social interaction problems, or to autistic people being 'obsessive' and set in their ways. In fact, for some of my participants, autism is *de facto* inherently problematic, and they listed behavioural difficulties, cognitive impairments, developmental delay and lack of empathy as some of the problems associated with autism.

Crucially, however, a good number of these same adults were also keen to point out that the child they worked with did not fit such a description, or in the case of the parents, that their offspring did not present in this way at all. The autistic children they knew were bright, funny, communicative and sociable, for example, a far cry from the 'persistent deficits in social communication and social interaction across multiple contexts' which we see in the DSM-5.[3] In other words, there was a disconnect between the authoritative, medical definitions of autism they might have unwittingly absorbed but felt unable to question, and the child they knew and, in the case of the parents especially, loved. It is hardly surprising, therefore, that many of my participants struggled to describe autism, just as you

---

3   See www.cdc.gov/ncbddd/autism/hcp-dsm.html

might feel confused if you really value a painting in an art gallery, but an art expert tells you it is deeply flawed.

As you will learn through the different chapters of this book, the very pervasiveness of these deficit-focused descriptions – even if they might contain some 'truths' – creates numerous difficulties for autistic children in schools and the people who try to support them. Furthermore, as you will see from the autistic contributors to this book, their understandings of autism and its manifestations might sometimes be at variance with each other, and so underscore the complexity – and indeed richness – of this phenomenon we call 'autism'.

■ It is a set of behaviours that can be observed and graded by an outside observer but that doesn't really tell us much about what it's like to be autistic and therefore what autism actually is. (Kabie)

What 'causes' autism?

An important consequence of classifying autism as a disease, a disorder and an abnormality is that people quite naturally want to find its causes. Perhaps unsurprisingly, therefore, the field of autism research in genetics, for example, is vast, and attracts huge amounts of funding (Pellicano, Dinsmore and Charman 2013), and can be characterised by complex projects involving multiple academics and institutions (see, for example, Mercati *et al.* 2017 and Pilorge *et al.* 2016). Indeed, according to Sweileh *et al.* (2016, p.1480), 'molecular genetics of ASD [autism spectrum disorder] is the primary hot topic' of autism research, as is the quest to find the elusive 'autism phenotype' (Lundström *et al.* 2015).

Much research has also been dedicated to the associated area of cognitive impairments. Here, the aim is typically to find an explanation for certain posited dysfunctions associated with autism, which can very briefly be summarised as follows:

• Mind-blindness: the inability to put oneself mentally in the position of another person (Baron-Cohen, Leslie and Frith 1985).

- Weak central coherence: a difficulty in understanding the general meaning of information rather than focusing on individual details (Briskman, Frith and Happé 2001).

- Poor executive function: an inability to regulate and control cognitive processes (Happé *et al.* 2006; Rosenthal *et al.* 2013).

Some debate surrounds the extent to which these theories can either individually or jointly provide an explanation for the supposed impairments associated with autism. Rajendran and Mitchell (2007), for example, conclude that because the three main cognitive theories have never been found to fully explain autism, it must therefore be a 'multi-deficit' disorder, a perspective they describe as 'intrinsically alluring' (2007, p.224). However, in an excellent study by Dawson *et al.* (2007), the authors explain how such research might be based unquestioningly on the notion that autism is 'characterized by cognitive impairment' (2007, p.657), whereby manifestations of ability are simply misinterpreted as additional signs of dysfunction rather than valid signs of intelligence. In other words, all aspects of autistic cognition can be problematised, and some research simply sets out to find answers to these unchallenged beliefs, creating a vicious cycle whereby autism will always emerge as a deficit. The fact remains that despite the vast amount of research in this area, no single 'autism gene' has ever been identified (Happé, Ronald and Plomin 2006). Indeed, some have questioned the ultimate purpose of autism research in genetics, and argue that projects of this nature are connected to eugenics (Arnold 2010), meaning that the ultimate aim would be to 'eliminate' autistic people.

And so, we still don't really know what 'causes' autism, or even if this is the question we should be asking. Nevertheless, there is a growing awareness across the broader research community that some of the traits and characteristics associated with autism should not necessarily be cast as impairments (Baron-Cohen *et al.* 2009a; Happé and Frith 2006), and that a more nuanced approach to autism research is required, involving more autistic people as co-partners, for example.

Interventions

This quest to find causes and explanations – the aetiology – of autism has also triggered the development of numerous 'interventions' designed to diminish autistic 'symptoms' and behaviours, or perhaps 'cure' autism altogether. Indeed, the notion of 'interventions', especially if they come 'early' (Boyd *et al.* 2010), is deeply rooted in the psyches of educators, parents, autism practitioners and the like. The UK charity Research Autism,[4] for example, lists well over a thousand 'interventions, treatments and therapies' designed to improve the functioning of the autistic individual, although the charity is careful to clarify that they endorse none, while some are deemed to be either 'scientifically unfeasible' or even 'potentially harmful'.

Examples of specific techniques include the Treatment and Education of Autistic Children with Communication Handicaps (TEACCH) (Mesibov and Howley 2003) and corrective strategies to facilitate a child's learning and inclusion in educational settings (Crosland and Dunlap 2012). Some advocate therapeutic input (Drahota *et al.* 2010), strategies to support communication and social interaction (McConnell 2002) and peer-mediated interventions (Chan *et al.* 2009), while others focus on the input of parents (Pickles *et al.* 2016).

In addition, Early Intensive Behavioural Intervention (EIBI) and other procedures addressing the issue of behaviour (Fava *et al.* 2012; Remington *et al.* 2007) are relatively widespread, with the highly disputed Applied Behaviour Analysis (ABA) perhaps the best known (Matson *et al.* 2012). However, the evidence base for the longer-term benefits of interventions is by no means clear or convincing (Kovshoff, Hastings and Remington 2011; Parsons *et al.* 2011), and some have questioned whether they are even needed at all (Milton 2014a).

Moreover, pursuits that in any other context might not appear under the banner of 'interventions' end up being labelled as such in the case of autistic children. Indeed, there is, in my view, an unhelpful tendency to co-opt the leisure activities and interests of autistic children in the name of therapeutic input. This applies to LEGO®, for example, which my contributor George is especially

---

4   www.researchautism.net

interested in, as are a number of autistic children and adults. This has led to the development of 'LEGO® therapy' (Owens *et al.* 2008), where the social skills of autistic children are deemed to improve as a result of structured activities using LEGO®. However, as will be discussed in Chapter 5, there are other ways of responding to the interests of autistic children without pathologising them or turning them into an intervention. In my view, interventions are a highly problematic concept as far is autism is concerned, because it is extremely difficult to measure their impact (Brignell *et al.* 2018), and when they don't 'work' (as often they don't), it's easy to then somehow blame the child. Not only this, but as Milton (2014a) has argued, sometimes interventions can be set up to problematise and change what might be perfectly innocuous traits which are an important part of someone's sense of identity.

Most of what I have discussed so far could be described as emanating from the 'medical model' of autism, sometimes called the 'individual model', where the basic premise is that a disabled person has problems and impairments that must be remedied in some way. In schools, this can result in a 'within-child' assessment of difficulty, as any problems experienced by an autistic child are considered to be a result of autism, rather than issues to do with the environment or a lack of understanding from others, for example. In fact, there is more than one type of medical model (Rioux and Valentine 2006), but nevertheless, they all converge on the notion that the dysfunctional individual somehow has a 'spoiled identity' (Williams and Mavin 2012), with some sense of 'normality' as a measure against which this person is failing (Hurst 2000). Let us now turn to alternative ways of conceptualising and describing autism.

Autism as 'difference'

It's not unusual to encounter descriptions of autism as a form of 'difference' and indeed, I have employed this notion myself in the past. This idea takes us away from the impairment model of autism, repositioning it as a variant of the human condition, at odds, perhaps, with the norm, but not a disorder. For example, Wittemeyer *et al.* (2011a), in the Professional Competency Framework that was produced on behalf of the Autism Education Trust (AET),[5] describe autism as 'a term used to describe a neurological difference in brain development that has a marked effect on how a person develops' (2011a, p.12). The authors set out 'four areas of difference' for educators to consider as they build their understanding of autism, and this conceptualisation – in which the habitual term 'disorder' appears to have been swapped for 'difference' – ushers us away from the notion that the child is somehow damaged and in need of repair. And so, embedded in a framework potentially enabling staff to understand better how to support autistic children and further their participation in school, the notion of 'difference' here suggests understanding, acceptance and inclusion.

 Autism is a neurological difference. I think I used to find it much easier to define but as I've learnt more it has become harder for me to 'pin down'. (Kabie)

Furthermore, Lawson (2008) presents a compelling case that autism is, in fact, a different form of ability – a 'diffability' – an alternative way of thinking and communicating, rather than a disposition defined by impairments. Lawson (2011) has therefore argued for a need to understand and embrace the thinking styles of autistic people. Baron-Cohen (2002a) also deliberates whether Asperger's syndrome 'should necessarily be viewed as a disability or, from a difference perspective, as a difference' (2002a, p.181). Consequently, describing autism as a form of 'difference' can be an important step in repositioning – or perhaps jettisoning – the impairment narrative around autism.

 It's different ways of thinking and going about things, a different sense of humour, a stronger interest in certain subjects. It makes you different in the way that you think. Not different like e.g. gender. Our differences make us human. (George)

 I use a lot of different thinking, different sensory perception in my artwork. (Jon)

---

5   www.autismeducationtrust.org.uk

On closer inspection, however, the idea of 'difference' can be seen as problematic. Just think about how you would feel if you were described as 'different'. If you're a funky, alternative sort of person, you might welcome this, but if you're more of a conventional type, preferring to not stand out in any way, such a description might worry you. Humphrey and Lewis (2008), for example, found mixed views from some autistic pupils in terms of how much they wanted to blend in with the general cohort or the extent to which they might be proud of their 'differences'. According to Ravet (2011), the notion of autism as a form of 'difference' might create a potential difficulty of 'norm referencing', raising the question of 'different to what?' In other words, if we are marking some people out as 'different', who are the 'normal' people we are measuring them against?

In fact, for some, the very notion of difference is entirely unhelpful, as it is 'constructed through binaries, with one being the norm, and also superior' (Williams and Mavin 2012, p.161). Liasidou (2012, p.26) refers to the 'individual deficit model of pathology and difference', while for Allan (2008, p.21), standards for inclusion create 'a problem and a spectacle of difference, to be managed and tolerated' by trainee teachers in particular. In my own study, many of the participants felt autistic people were 'different', but while for some this was a positive attribute, for others it had connotations of strangeness, oddity and weirdness. Therefore, to separate some people out as 'different', however well intended, might, in fact, serve to stigmatise and exclude, rather than value and include.

> Lessons that talk about disabled people or try to spread autism awareness or try to educate about any difference, can do more harm than good: this approach relies upon seeing some children as 'other' rather than part of a whole that makes up the global population. (Kabie)

In educational contexts, this quandary, which centres on whether or not it is helpful to identify certain individuals as 'different', has been termed the 'dilemma of difference' (Norwich 2008; Terzi 2005). Acknowledging certain children as being 'different', perhaps requiring alternative curricula, teaching techniques and even educational placements, might mean that they receive the support they require, but at the same time this can result in unhelpful labelling and exclusion. On the other hand, not identifying some children in this way could mean they are in some senses more accepted and included, but denied the provision of much-needed assistance.

So you can see the problem with describing autism as a form of 'difference' and the dilemmas this creates. Therefore, we must proceed with caution when employing the notion of 'difference' in the context of autism, and make sure we consult with those to whom it might be applied. Indeed, Norwich (2008) ends his book by quoting one of his participants, a disabled teenager, who says that sometimes he wants to be treated the same as everyone else, sometimes differently, but that he likes to be asked.

'Othering'

For Williams and Mavin (2012), constructing an individual as 'different' is akin to 'othering', a point my contributor Kabie also made in her previous comment. 'Othering' has been described by Hughes (2009, p.686) as the process whereby 'the normal' and 'the pathological' are separated, with disabled people occupying the undesirable space of 'other'. Therefore, even if the concept of 'difference' might be useful in certain contexts and from some perspectives, being 'othered' is not. Indeed, according to Williams and Mavin (2012), 'othering' is inevitably accompanied by exclusionary attitudes and practices.

Milton (2012a, p.885) also describes the stigma of being 'othered' or 'defined as abnormal', which can mean that certain individuals are 'socially stigmatised, shunned and sanctioned'. For Milton and Sims (2016, p.526), societal 'othering' can lead to autistic people experiencing 'problems with authority figures (expectations of obedience and conformity), stigma and bullying'. Indeed, the issue does not solely apply to disabled people: in 1949 Simone de Beauvoir identified how women occupy the place of 'the Other', and subsequent feminist writers such as Joan Kelly-Gadol (1987) have also explored how women have always been a socially oppressed group, defined by a sense of 'otherness'. And in schools, too often children with SEND can be perceived as being 'not like us' (Davis, Watson and Cunningham-Burley 2000, p.209), and so not provided with the same opportunities as their peers.

Neurodiversity

As we have seen, the notion of 'difference' is complex and carries both positive and negative connotations, creating dilemmas for educators. Meanwhile, certain categories of people can be 'othered', positioned as 'not normal' and deviant. Lawson (2008), however, sheds light on these questions by arguing that the 'ideal' of inclusion could be 'a reality for many during school years if difference was fostered as part of being normal' (2008, p.96). For Lawson (2008), the whole issue rests on our very concept of normality, and the need to recognise 'diversity and difference as part of everyday normal or typical life' (2008, p.26). In other words, the problem is not so much about 'difference', how it might be defined or even whether it is a helpful concept, but our very understanding of normality, which, being particularly narrow, means that certain people inevitably fall outside of its limited parameters. According to Lawson (2008), therefore, it is this very narrow conceptualisation of normality that restricts, excludes or potentially disables 'others'.

This leads us to the notion of diversity, or perhaps 'neurodiversity' (Ekblad 2013; Kapp *et al.* 2013), which potentially provides a more meaningful and inclusive description of the various manifestations of autism than 'difference'. This term, originally coined by Singer in 1997/1998, is considered to facilitate a greater acceptance of autism in its diverse manifestations (Nolan and McBride 2015), as well as other dispositions or conditions, whether or not they are accompanied by impairments. Situated in relation to 'neurotypicality', the concept of neurodiversity could potentially offer a solution to the dilemmas of difference and the problem of 'othering' already described.

■ Autism is an innate way of thinking. We're a variation on humanity's wonderful diversity. Nowadays what would really help is an understanding that neurodiversity is just another form of being human, and not broken. (Jon)

■ Autism is part of natural neurodiversity, a neurodivergence amongst many (I remain unconvinced of a true neurotypical majority). (Kabie)

Whatever your own view, it seems clear that we need to move away from the impairment-focused, medicalised descriptions of autism summarised at the start of this chapter, or the idea that autism can be narrowly defined as being on 'a spectrum' (Happé 2015; Lawson 2011). Indeed, according to Grinker (2015, p.345), to emphasise solely medical understandings of autism is to fail to recognise the intrinsic value of autistic people and the ways in which they 'contribute to human diversity and creativity'.

Is autism a disability?

Now that we have wrestled with the big beasts of questions around autism prevalence, diagnosis, genetic research, interventions, difference and diversity, let us now turn to the thorny issue of whether autism is a disability. If you know autistic people, or are autistic, you might already have strong views on this, placing you in one camp or another. So I'm going to put this very simply and say: *it depends.*

Earlier, we touched briefly on issues around the medical model of autism and disability, where any difficulties, impairments and dysfunctions an individual possesses are considered to be inherent to that person. This model is the founding stone of how many understand autism and SEND generally, underpinning a whole raft of educational, administrative and social policies for disabled children and adults (Molloy and Vasil 2002; Slee and Allan 2001). As we have already seen, many accounts present autism as a suite of deficiencies, and any difficulties in school, for example, are a result of 'ASD-related manifestations' (Emam and Farrell 2009, p.407). Therefore, problems autistic children might be experiencing in class, and difficulties teachers have in teaching them, are essentially considered to be a result of the fact that they are autistic. And this applies no matter how well intentioned school staff might be, or how strong their desire to be understanding and inclusive.

However, there is an alternative model – the social model – with which a number of readers may already be familiar. Again, there is more than one type of social model, but essentially this model suggests that disablement is derived not from the individual inherently, but from the limitations of societal structures and attitudes which create barriers and difficulties for certain people. It's a highly complex area of discussion, with debates around the issue of impairment, for example (Allan 2010), and some commentators offering more interactional models (Shakespeare 2014) or biopsychosocial models. It is certainly worth taking a moment to consider whether or not our current school systems and structures – bearing in mind that at least 1 in 100 children are autistic – were ever designed with autistic children in mind (Wood 2016). Terzi (2005, p.446), for example, is of the view that the medical model as played out in educational environments results in 'perspectives emphasising individual limitations' rather than the ways in which the organisation and design of schools might create those very difficulties in the first instance.

■ Autism is not a disability. Apart from the ones that society has put in the way – there are no disadvantages. (George)

■ I hesitate to call it a gift – it has been for me. But it's not for everyone, so it's good to be on the cautious side. (Jon)

■ I identify as a disabled person because in a society which is mainly non-autistic my needs often aren't accommodated. I am disabled by a neuronormative world and have been since I was born. (Kabie)

■ Autism is a lifelong, developmental condition that affects the way a person communicates and relates to others around them. (Michael)

In fact, for Liasidou (2012, p.5), the concept of inclusive education, if it is to be meaningful, is necessarily founded on the social model, as it 'refers to the restructuring of social and, by implication, educational settings in order to meet the needs of all learners irrespective of their diverse biographical, developmental and learning trajectories'. Within this framework, we are not expecting autistic children to change their very being or nature, but are aiming instead to ensure that the buildings, curriculum, classroom layout and teaching styles will be able to accommodate them. Therefore, this issue runs deeper than, say, providing a sensory room or differentiated learning materials, but impacts on all aspects of how an autistic child is perceived, addressed and supported. This approach can be facilitated through 'universal design' (Liasidou 2012; Woronko and Killoran 2011), where every aspect of educational provision is planned from scratch to accommodate a diversity of learners. In this way, certain children are not identified as needing adjustments or adaptations, but the core design of the curriculum, classroom layout and buildings means that all learners are more naturally accommodated – idealistic, perhaps, but surely worth a try.

> I tend to follow a social model, that society puts the barriers up to me – that's the impairment I have. A lot of people talk about mental issues and autism. I steadfastly say that the mental health issues come from people's lack of understanding. People tend to conflate the two. I don't see it as a disability; I see people's attitude towards me as being a disability. (Jon)

Moreover, if all of the strategies, techniques and interventions a school might put in place rest on the core belief that autism is a problematic condition that they must try to alleviate, then any failures will necessarily be deemed to result from the problem of 'autism' itself. It is this very belief – for indeed it is a matter of unquestioned faith for some – that arguably lies at the heart of the general failure of autistic children to thrive in schools. Think of the beautiful painting you saw in the art gallery. You were told it was flawed, and so you believed it. But what if a thousand people came forward and said to the art expert: 'No, you're looking at it from a particular perspective. Look at it differently, and you'll see its many qualities.' So is autism a disability? Well yes, if you fail to understand and accommodate autistic people, if you expect them to slot into the status quo, regardless of their needs, wishes and particular dispositions. If children spend their educational life being essentially told, one way or another, that they are flawed, damaged goods, then this may well result in a disabling lack of self-confidence, or serious mental health issues in later life.

> People's non-understanding of autism is a disability, along with some experts, the way they've written about autism. (Jon)

Nevertheless, and this is a crucial point, it doesn't mean that autistic children don't need help or support. Indeed, some require a great deal in areas such as communication, sensory issues (Bogdashina 2016), motor problems (Downey and Rapport 2012), alexithymia (a difficulty in recognising one's own emotions: see

Shah *et al.* 2016), self-organisation, Tourette's (Baron-Cohen *et al.* 1999) or anxiety (Grondhuis and Aman 2012). Pathological Demand Avoidance (PDA) has also been associated with autism, although its existence as a separate syndrome is not proved (Green *et al.* 2018), and some question whether PDA constitutes a distinct set of identifiable behaviours (Woods 2017). Even so, these issues are not purely socially constructed, and they might be inherently disabling, although their severity is greatly increased if they are not recognised and supported.

It's worth remembering too that we all experience disability, one way or another, at some point in our lifetime, be it through accident, illness or old age. As Pfeiffer (2000) said, disability is on a continuum; there is not a clear demarcation between 'able' and 'disabled'. Rather, it is a complex interplay between our own particular dispositions and the support and opportunities we are given. And if your starting point with an autistic child is that they are inherently impaired, then you are immediately disabling that child by your very attitude alone, and no good can come of it.

Does it mainly affect boys?

In a word, *no*. This is despite the fact that studies on autism prevalence show that many more boys than girls are autistic. Taylor, Jick and MacLaughlin (2013), for example, found autism diagnoses occurred more in boys than girls, at a rate of approximately 3:1, while Brugha *et al.* (2011), using survey data of adults in England, established that 1.8 per cent of men had a diagnosis of autism compared with a mere 0.2 per cent of women. Baron-Cohen *et al.* (2009b) asserted that 1 in 66 boys aged between 5 and 9 were autistic, compared with 1 in 208 girls.

Baron-Cohen (2002b) also posited the theory that autism is a manifestation of the 'extreme male brain', although he is careful to point out that this does not mean only men can be autistic. Nevertheless, if you read research papers about autism that involve autistic participants in some way or another, it's worth checking how many females were involved. A number of major studies have either very few or no female participants at all (see, for example, Mawhood, Howlin and Rutter 2000), suggesting a somewhat vicious cycle of male-focused research that fails to consider the impact of autistic women on findings.

There is a great deal of discussion as to why there is this imbalance of gender, with attitudes slowly shifting towards a sense that current diagnostic processes and criteria do not capture the ways in which autism might be manifested in girls and women (Gould 2017; Gould and Ashton-Smith 2011). Some have argued that this lack of recognition has resulted in years of difficulties and struggle, where women have been misunderstood and misdiagnosed, creating numerous problems in their lives (Hendrickx 2015; Lawson 2014). There is also a developing view that autistic women are more prone to 'mask' or camouflage their autistic traits (Cook, Ogden and Winstone 2017; Hull *et al.* 2017), the effort of which can itself impact on their mental health (Hendrickx 2015).

Indeed, this whole area of research, which has increased exponentially over recent years, is very much in its infancy. These issues are highly relevant to any considerations of what autism *is*, since new understandings about how autism might be manifested in women necessarily create a shift in our understanding of autism overall (Stewart 2016). Furthermore, while it is important that autism diagnoses are not dominated by a 'male model', we must, in my view, avoid essentialising autism as far as gender is concerned. In other words, I consider that creating a blanket 'this is how autism is manifested in girls, and this is how it is manifested in boys' dichotomy is unhelpful (see Chapter 10 on issues concerning gender fluidity, non-binary identification and diversity).

Interestingly, Dr Catriona Stewart, who has a diagnosis of autism herself, provided the following comment for this book, challenging the idea that autistic women have somehow been invisible until recent times:

> Before girls/women were recognised in research...autistic people who were writing books, giving presentations – they were mostly women. Liane Holliday Willey published her first book in 1999, Claire Sainsbury's was 2000, Ros Blackburn was doing the speaking rounds during the 90s and 2000s, Genevieve Edmunds... So autistic women theoretically didn't really figure but they actually were there in full view!

Terminology

Which terminology to use in relation to autism is an issue that can cause a great deal of debate and even acrimony. Moreover, just as ideas about autism and gender are evolving, so, too, are ideas about how to refer to autistic people, such as whether to use 'person first' (e.g. child with autism) or 'identity first' (e.g. autistic child) language. The general consensus from autistic adults seems to be that they prefer the latter (Kenny *et al.* 2016; Sinclair 1999). This is because being autistic, for many, is not perceived as an 'add-on' but rather, a valued and essential part of their being. For these reasons, I use 'identity first' language in the book. In addition, I also avoid functioning labels – 'high' and 'low' – as these can be misleading and unhelpful (Dawson 2010).

Crucially – and this point is often missed – there are some important parallels between debates around the medical and social models in relation to autism and the thorny question of terminology. Terms such as autistic spectrum disorder (ASD) tend to derive from the medical/impairment model of autism and so I do not use them in the book (unless I am quoting someone who does). This has been replaced in some quarters by autistic spectrum condition/s (ASC), but it's not clear if 'condition' is much better (Broderick and Ne'eman 2008), since it evokes notions of medical conditions, for example, so I no longer use this either. While it is undoubtedly the case that there are divergent viewpoints within the broader autism community (Kenny *et al.* 2016), there is nevertheless a gradual shift away from an impairment focus and its incumbent vocabulary towards greater emphasis on the strengths that can be associated with autism.

- Disorder – it's medical language and it's saying that we're broken. As a child I was continually told that I was broken. When you live with that, when you're told you're broken, as a child, you believe it, especially when you're told you're supposed to believe adults. (Jon)

- People often refer to autism as a disorder, which is very negative in my opinion. It's more often than not that people don't know how to effectively communicate with autistic people. More positive (or at least neutral) terminology should be the norm and a shift away from it being a disorder needs to happen. (Michael)

In addition, there are also conflicting views on whether or not 'Asperger's' (and 'Aspie') should continue to be used in light of the fact that the DSM-5 (APA 2013) no longer includes this as a category (Giles 2013; Linton *et al.* 2013). Indeed, this has been complicated further by recent reports in the press linking Hans Asperger himself with Nazi Germany.

I tend to use 'autism' as a blanket term, but employ 'Asperger's' if an individual has used it or it is referenced in an article or book. It's an issue that matters a great deal to some autistic people, and the basic lesson is that we should be careful to respect their wishes as to how they would like to be addressed and described. And bear in mind, of course, that some autistic people do not like to identify as such at all.

■ Autism or autistic – because the word itself has no negative connotations as would come with words such as 'disorder'. I use both autistic person and person with autism, sometimes in the same sentence. (George)

■ I don't use person first. I'm an autistic person. I think if you say 'with autism' or 'suffers from' (I suffer from people's attitudes), it engenders a distance, a separation. You wouldn't say 'there's a man with gayness'. (Jon)

■ I am an autistic person, I reject ideas of autism as an appendage or an 'add-on'. It isn't something that I 'have' or can leave behind if I choose to. I refer you to Jim Sinclair's 'Why I don't like "person first" language' which reflects my views very well. (Kabie)

Conclusion

In this, the first and longest chapter of the book, I have only been able to cover briefly the extremely complex issue of how autism is described and defined. As we have seen, autism may well be a result of a person's genetic make-up, but it seems unlikely that there is a single 'autism gene'. Moreover, autistic children in schools may require support with communication and sensory issues, for example, but these difficulties might be significantly reduced in the right environment, particularly if the principles of universal design are adopted. Indeed, if autistic children are accepted as part of the diversity of pupils who populate a school, they are much less likely to appear as 'different', or to experience disablement.

Key points

- While it is difficult to define autism, educators and researchers need to reflect carefully and critically on their own understandings of autism before embarking on any kind of programme involving autistic children or adults.

- In school settings, these understandings about autism need to be shared by all those working with a particular child.

- The assumption should not be made that an autistic child is impaired, and consideration should be given to the range of factors which might impact on how that child is able to function in school.

- An autistic child might need help, but so might many other children too. Any support provided should not stigmatise and further exclude the autistic child.

- Educational interventions should be rigorously evaluated in terms of whether or not they genuinely benefit an individual child.

- The individual wishes of the autistic person in terms of how they would like to be described should be respected.

Chapter 2

Sensory Issues

Introduction

One of the more encouraging developments in the autism field over the last decade or so has been a growing awareness of the significance of sensory issues. Sensory sensitivities are included in the DSM-5 as part of the diagnostic criteria for autism, and in teacher training materials, such as those provided by the AET. They are also highlighted in campaigns by the National Autistic Society (NAS), for example.

But despite these signs of increased understanding, I'm not convinced that in our schools there is a sufficiently nuanced appreciation of this multi-faceted phenomenon, which potentially influences a whole range of physical and perceptual processes (Bogdashina 2016). Indeed, the school environment can present autistic children with a multi-sensory onslaught in terms of sounds, smells, textures and visual impacts that constitutes both a distraction and a source of discomfort (Ashburner, Ziviani and Rodger 2008; Caldwell 2008). There was also clear evidence from my own study that sensory issues, and noise in particular, can be highly exclusionary factors for autistic children in schools.

While it's a very complex area, and not one I could possibly do full justice to here, in this chapter I try to unpick some common misconceptions about sensory issues and autism, such as the confusion with the 'sensory stage' of development, and suggest how this misunderstanding can impact on the education of autistic children. In addition, I focus on the issues that most stood out during my research: namely, noise, space and visual clutter.

It's also important to understand that sensory sensitivities can be associated with abilities and strengths, so I also consider the positive aspects of these predispositions, and touch briefly on autism and synaesthesia.

The complexity of sensory issues

As many readers will be aware, sensory sensitivities might operate in relation to sound, sight, touch, smell or taste. Perhaps fewer will be familiar with proprioception (which concerns an awareness of one's body in space), or know about the vestibular system (which potentially impacts on a person's sense of balance). Autistic children and adults can be susceptible to difficulties in all of these areas (Caldwell 2008), underscoring how multi-faceted this whole phenomenon is. Autistic people can be highly sensitive – hypersensitive – and need to avoid bright lights, for example, or they might be in some respects under-sensitive – hyposensitive – and require additional input, such as in the form of deep pressure.

Indeed, the same person can be both hyper and hyposensitive, as these states are not fixed, but fluctuate according to both external and internal circumstances (Bogdashina 2016). For example, the autistic writer Donna Williams (1992/1999, p.9) described autism as:

...an internal human 'normality' with the volume turned up. We all have experienced moments when we aren't quite aware or when we are too aware to handle the world... We all have had times when we've had hardly any awareness of our bodies, even been out of them, or felt so in, weighed down by them, that we become hypercritical, eager to escape, tune out, disappear.

As Williams (1992/1999) suggests, these issues have been linked to difficulties in recognising internal bodily states such as hunger and temperature (interoception). They are also associated with an inability to understand one's own emotions (alexithymia) and anorexia (Merwin *et al.* 2013). Problems such as face-blindness (prosopagnosia) and disorders of vision such as scotopic sensitivity may also come under the broad umbrella of sensory and perceptual complexities associated with autism (Bogdashina 2016).

- Smells, cleaning fluids and art materials; poster paint has a really awful smell and Plasticine® made me feel sick. Working with clay: it feels horrible on my hands when it starts to dry. School uniform, itchy and uncomfortable, it sometimes made it difficult to concentrate. At my school, only boys could wear trousers and I hate the skin on skin feel of legs under a skirt, it makes me feel sick and it becomes impossible to concentrate. Scraping furniture: chairs scraping against a non-carpeted floor. The fire alarm. Having to hold hands with other children. Music lessons: lots of people making random noises that sounded a mess. (Kabie)

- Sometimes it actually stinks in my classroom and no one notices it apart from me. (Rose, 8)

As well as making autistic children feel ill at ease or even physically unwell, these phenomena can also be upsetting and frightening, and yet this is happening within the very environment in which their learning is supposed to be taking place. It's like being asked to walk into the middle of a fireworks display and being made to sit down and concentrate on some quantum mechanics.

- When I think back I get an overwhelming feeling of stuffy heat, closeness, a claustrophobic-type trapped feeling. (Kabie)

Sensory issues and development

Developmental psychology is a complex field beyond the scope of my own research, although its influence is ever-present. Indeed, framing the ways in which children grow, adapt and learn as they increase in age as a phenomenon that progresses on the basis of 'development' and in 'developmental stages' is extremely pervasive. Autism itself is often conceived of as a 'developmental disorder' (see, for example, Robins *et al.* 2001), with autistic children considered to be 'developmentally delayed' (De Giacomo and Fombonne 1998), or to have a 'spikey profile' (Happé 1994), meaning that they have strengths in some areas, but not in others. Therefore, it's worth taking a moment to consider how this perception might impact on the ways in which educators interpret the sensory sensitivities of autistic children.

The idea that children develop in 'stages', and that they must reach each of these 'milestones' before they can progress to the next, is considered to derive from the pioneering Swiss clinical psychologist Jean Piaget (Lloyd-Smith and Tarr 2000), amongst others (Evans 2017). The earliest of these is the 'sensorimotor stage', often reduced, colloquially, to 'the sensory stage', and is considered an important precursor to language development (Curcio 1978). However, autistic children, well beyond early infancy, might feel drawn to items that have a strong sensory appeal, and respond to their environment by touching, smelling and placing items to their lips, for example. Unfortunately, this can be interpreted erroneously as a sign that they are somehow 'stuck' in the 'sensory stage' and that they are 'developmentally delayed'. As a result, unjustified assumptions can be made about their understanding and maturity, or the level of academic work they are able to access.

Indeed, children don't, as such, 'grow out of' these dispositions, which may well extend across the lifespan (Crane, Goddard and Pring 2009; Williams 1998), even while the autistic person is learning and maturing in other ways. Temple Grandin, for example, a professor of animal science and also autistic, described how as a teenager she would position herself in the squeeze chute on her aunt's ranch, normally used to hold cattle in place, in order to achieve the proprioceptive pressure she required (BBC Science & Nature 2006). This example underscores how different types of sensory input are a deep necessity, and that if children in school are denied this, they might spend their whole day feeling out of kilter, and unable to concentrate and learn. Therefore, an interest in sensory items may well have little to do with development, but rather tell us something about how that child learns and responds to their environment.

Moreover, the continued association of sensory needs with developmental delay means that physical items used by all children in the early stages of education – bead strings, weighing scales, clocks, number lines, etc. – are expected to be discarded as the child progresses academically. However, the particular sensory and cognitive dispositions of some children may mean that physical items are needed to support learning well beyond the early stages of primary school, without this being an indication that the child is somehow not making progress. Indeed, as the comment below from Jon indicates, autistic children might have a particular, emotional attachment to certain objects that they even personify (White and Remington 2018), and so removing them from an autistic child should always be approached with caution.

As a young child, I remember, picking up stones from the garden – they had personality, they had feelings, they had life. Like plants – and other objects. I grew up with this being natural to me – which is why I become a geologist. I think a lot of autistic people have this. A stone doesn't let you down – what you see is what you get. I had a Corky the Cat balloon – I carried it around for three weeks until it popped. I felt bereft. I can relate to those feelings now. I can compare this with when my mother died. I made a card of fossils that I found, but it was thrown out. I had a complete meltdown. I had to go and retrieve it. They were my pals. They were part of my universe. (Jon)

In addition, a vague notion about sensory needs might mean that autistic children, willy-nilly and regardless of whether or not their individual disposition dictates this, can be presented with squeeze balls, flashing lights and other sensory toys by well-intentioned school staff, determined to provide some sort of sensory input. In fact, this kind of blanket approach to sensory needs may well do more harm than good, running the risk of frustrating or even overloading the child.

Therefore, school staff should try to avoid a judgemental and generalised approach towards sensory needs and dispositions, an understanding of which plays an important part in the effective inclusion of autistic children in school.

Too much noise

We already know that schools can be noisy places, both internally and externally (Shield and Dockrell 2004), and this was my subjective impression when I was collecting data (Wood 2018a). A great deal of din came from the classroom, such as with the scraping of chairs and tables, or the repeated instructions of teachers, as well as the chatter from children. The racket also emanated from elsewhere in the school, especially during breaks and lunchtimes, when the norm seemed to be a lot of running around and shouting and screaming.

This is a lot to deal with for children who are very sensitive to noise and other sensorial impacts, or who might have difficulties in processing language (Klatte, Bergström and Lachmann 2013). Indeed, excessive noise has been shown to have a negative impact on the reading ability and language development of pupils with SEND (Klatte *et al.* 2013; Woolner and Hall 2010). Dockrell and Shield (2006) also found that schoolchildren with SEND performed significantly worse on most measures in different noise conditions, and that the 'babble' of other children had a particularly detrimental effect on them. In other words, the talking of other children can have a deleterious effect on the communication of children with language impairments.

Indeed, autistic children can be especially susceptible to excessive noise in schools (Jones *et al.* 2008; Menzinger and Jackson 2009), even more than other pupils with SEND. These sorts of impacts can be overwhelming (Batten *et al.* 2006) and interfere with their ability to process language (Bogdashina 2016).

■ The library, where I spend almost all of my break/lunchtimes, is often busy and loud because of boys in older year groups misbehaving and causing a lot of trouble. (Grace, 14)

■ Going to kids' parties – kids screaming and the noise, I was very sensitive to noise. There was a local factory – a crisp factory, and they did kids' parties – hell. Also Saturday morning cinema viewings – kids screaming. (Jon)

■ Noise was difficult, particularly in the gym doing PE and at lunchtimes in the dining hall and in the playground. (Kabie)

Some of the children in my study, much like the contributors to this book, were very negatively impacted by excessive noise levels in school, meaning that they had to miss certain lessons and other activities, or even go home for part of the day. This was despite the fact that being in control of noise was important to the teachers, who employed various techniques such as rhythmic clapping, tambourine tapping, getting the children to sit cross-legged on the floor with a finger placed on their lips, or even to 'freeze' in the playground if they needed their attention (Wood 2018a).

Needless to say, the dining hall, as well as being busy, crowded and a source of multiple odours, was also very noisy, as trays were picked up and clattered back down, cutlery jangled, and metal serving dishes clanged against metal hot plates. Meanwhile, the children, squeezed into rows of tiny seats bolted on to collapsible dining tables, grew louder and louder to make themselves heard over the racket. Indeed, the lunch queue alone can be the place where sensory problems 'can turn into a nightmare' (Sainsbury 2009, p.99). Perhaps unsurprisingly, therefore, all of the child contributors to this book – Grace, James, Rose and Zack – identified noise and crowds as being the most difficult aspects of school from a sensory point of view.

■ The queues in the canteen at lunch are huge and it takes ages to get my food and I am very claustrophobic, so the crowds can be stressful to me. (Grace, 14)

■ I always found lunchtimes very hard because there was a lot of noise. (Jon)

■ I did have to eat my lunch in the dining hall and that wasn't great; so noisy. Getting jostled in the queue, having to be so close to other people, the smell. (Kabie)

Given these circumstances, we must also consider the impact on autistic children who might be seated with a teaching assistant (TA) to one side of the main cohort while the rest of the class is noisily engaged with some other activity. Or they might be working on alternative targets with a TA in the busy corridor outside. This was certainly the case for some of the autistic children in my study, who therefore had to deal with more noise and distractions than their peers.

And, just to add a further layer of complexity to this issue, my research also revealed that it wasn't only loud noises that distracted the children, but 'quiet' ones too, such as the hum of an overhead strip light, or the buzzing of a fly, meaning that this is by no means a straightforward or easy issue for school staff to deal with. Nevertheless, in my view, noise is undoubtedly a potentially exclusionary phenomenon for autistic children in schools, and must be addressed on both an individualised and collective basis if solutions are to be found (Wood 2018a).

> I like going on holiday in the Lake District and going for long walks in the woods and parks where it's quiet. (Zack, 10)

A question of space

It's also useful to consider how much the problem of noise in schools might interlink with the question of space. For example, the staff in my study only resorted to one-to-one teaching in the school corridor because there was nowhere else to go. Indeed, in an ideal world, schools would have the space to accommodate a real diversity of learner needs and dispositions, with quiet rooms, secluded pods[1] for individual study, music and sensory rooms, a bespoke gym and art studio, for example. Outdoors, there would be plenty of space for games and to run around and shout, as well as quiet places for the more contemplative types.

But the reality is, in England at least, that primary schools are becoming increasingly more densely populated, while the spaces they occupy, in the broadest sense, are shrinking. In 2010,

---

1   Not to be confused with isolation booths, which are typically used as a form of punishment.

for example, 74 per cent of state primary schools had a population of 300 or fewer pupils, and a mere 16 had more than 800 pupils (DfE 2010). By 2017, only 62 per cent of primary schools had 300 or fewer pupils, and the number with over 800 pupils had risen to 122 (DfE 2017a). These are the so-called 'supersize' primary schools, many boosted by the mergers that have taken place countrywide of numerous infant and junior schools, made possible by the *Education and Inspections Act* (2006). This is potentially bad news for pupils with SEND, who may well be better supported in smaller schools (Humphrey and Squires 2011).

Interestingly, the picture for secondary schools, already typically much larger than primary schools, is more mixed, showing an increase in the number of schools with 300 or fewer pupils during the last decade, and a decrease in those with more than 800 pupils (DfE 2010, 2017a). In addition, and despite much debate about this in the media, class sizes, according to Department for Education (DfE) figures, have remained more or less stable during this time, with an average of 26/27 for primary schools and 20/21 for secondary schools, although infant school classes are the largest, often with 30 pupils (DfE 2017a).

Nevertheless, lack of space was evidently an issue in the schools involved in my own research. In one of the schools, for example, even the corridors had to be booked as 'rooms', with some staff freely admitting, in the labyrinthine layout of this densely populated school, that they didn't know where all the classrooms were. How is a child supposed to make sense of such an environment? In these circumstances, meeting the needs of a diversity of learners, and tackling the issue of noise, for example, is impeded simply because of a lack of space.

Moreover, school classrooms, already replete with numerous children, are expected to fulfil a multiplicity of functions, with reading corners, a carpet for group teaching, sinks to wash art materials, storage cupboards and IT equipment, for example. When I was collecting data, sometimes even PE lessons took place in the classroom, which was far from ideal. Meanwhile, a number of schools in England have disposed of their playing fields, suggesting a reduced emphasis on outdoor spaces for schoolchildren, and a failure to recognise the importance of exercise for physical and emotional well-being and academic attainment. Trudeau and

Shephard (2008), for example, found that unstructured physical activity could impact positively on concentration, memory and classroom behaviour. Similarly, Singh *et al.* (2012) found a significant longitudinal relationship between physical activity and academic performance.

We should return, therefore, to the concept of 'universal design', discussed briefly in the last chapter, which suggests that schools should be planned from the outset to include a diversity of learners. According to the United Nations (UN) *Convention on the Rights of Persons with Disabilities* (CRPD) (UN DESA 2006), for example, the idea of universal design refers to 'the design of products, environments, programmes and services to be usable by all people, to the greatest extent possible, without the need for adaptation or specialized design' (Article 2). Therefore, inclusion means more than simply adapting the environment, for example, but also concerns more fundamental changes that reduce the need for this to even be a necessary and active process. And so, even though the concept of 'universal design' is not only about use and availability of space, it certainly helps schools to be inclusive, and to fulfil the ideals of universal design, if they have plenty of it.

Visual clutter

If school classrooms are crowded and expected to house a range of activities, this does not preclude a tendency in the UK to have artwork and posters covering every inch of wall space, papier-mâché models perched on book cases and glittery murals dangling from the ceilings for extra visual impact. Even though some research suggests that background distractions are not necessarily a problem for autistic children and might not prevent them from engaging with core learning tasks (Remington *et al.* 2019), this phenomenon is generally considered to have a potentially overloading impact on autistic children who are already very sensitive sensorially.

When I enter a room, I see everything in the room – at once. In some scenarios this is awful, for example with a very 'busy' room that has much to take in, but I will be expected to engage with a professional or be alert and focused. I don't do well with bright lights, strip lights, electrical noises, manmade clutter. Even libraries can be difficult because although I love the old-style libraries packed with books, the myriad of pictures and words on the books and often extra info from posters, etc. can leave me unable to function well. (Kabie)

According to Alexander (2000, p.184), these showy displays are 'suggestive of ostentation, window dressing or peacockery', and are of minimal value educationally. Alexander (2000, p.176) also decries the fact that during the 1980s and 1990s there developed in the UK an 'institutionalized obsession' whereby more attention was paid to 'school décor, classroom organization and display' than learning. These attitudes, Alexander (2000) argues, were conflated and confused with principles of pedagogy and education. Indeed, there is no *law* that dictates classrooms have to be covered floor to ceiling in glitzy displays.

▨ I found the whole thing bewildering with how many different people there were, and the size of it, and the entire thing in general. Noise, and visual clutter. (George)

▨ Visual information overload: from all of the pictures on the walls/ strung across classrooms. (Kabie)

▨ Examining things on the wall or new surroundings were more interesting to me than what the teacher was saying. (Michael)

Therefore, if noise and lack of space reduce the inclusivity of schools, visual clutter can also be a significant contributory factor. Indeed, all children would surely benefit from fewer distractions during lessons, and to be working in a visually calmer environment (Woronko and Killoran 2011).

Sensory strengths and synaesthesia

So far, we have discussed the problems that can derive from sensory sensitivities and how they can be misunderstood, ignored or exacerbated. And it is the case that life can be difficult for autistic children and adults in a world that is so much brighter, busier and noisier than it used to be (Moudon 2009). However, setting aside the fact that we all, to an extent, derive some sort of sensory pleasure from the world, it would be completely misleading to simply problematise sensory sensitivities as far as autistic people are concerned. Not only can these sensitivities be the source of a great deal of contentment and provide a feeling of well-being, but this disposition is also associated with heightened perception, a profound visual and aural acuity (Mottron *et al.* 2013), artistic talent, and even intuition (Bogdashina 2010).

> You're able to pick up more from the world around you – you can see things and hear things that other people can't. It makes the world more interesting. It just opens up what's around you, what other people wouldn't obviously know of. (George)

Indeed, there are many autistic visual artists, musicians and writers. Temple Grandin and Donna Williams have both authored several books, as has Wenn Lawson, who wrote the Foreword to this book. Jon Adams, one of the contributors to this book, is a well-established artist, who writes poetry too. Michael Barton, another contributor, is a published author, and the illustrations in this book were created by the autistic artist Sonny Hallett. Similarly, Alan Gardner – more popularly known as 'The Autistic Gardener' – has made a success of designing gardens according to his unique insights and sensitivities. The point to underscore here is that some autistic people are not creative *despite* being autistic, but rather *because of* being autistic.

> I love art because I enjoy drawing as well as other things like oil pastels and painting with watercolours. Art is my passion. I love to draw and spend a lot of time doing it in and out of school, and animation is really fun. (Grace, 14)

> I love the outdoors, being emerged completely in birdsong and the sights, sounds and smells of trees in a forest is amazing, everything rushing at me at once and making me feel whole, as if I am a part of this nature that is pouring into me. I have a beech tree in my garden and the sound of that is amazing; I planted it as a seedling and it feels like a friend. (Kabie)

▨ Being particularly sensitive to something can be advantageous – whether it's picking out extra details in music or using auditory clues to diagnosing problems with a car, there are many situations where sensory sensitivity can be beneficial. (Michael)

▨ I'm quite good at smelling things. I can smell chips from about 50 metres away. (Rose, 8)

In some cases, autism is also associated with synaesthesia (Baron-Cohen *et al.* 2013) which, to put it very simply, is a phenomenon whereby one type of perception or sensation produces an impression involving other senses. For example, the autistic writer Daniel Tammet (2006) opens his autobiographical book, *Born on a Blue Day*, with the following words:

> I was born on 31 January 1979 – a Wednesday. I know it was on Wednesday, because the date is blue in my mind and Wednesdays are always blue, like the number nine or the sound of loud voices arguing. I like my birth date, because of the way I'm able to visualise most of the numbers in it as smooth and round shapes, similar to pebbles on a beach. (2006, p.1)

Tammet, whose exceptional abilities have been the source of much academic and scientific interest (see, for example, Bor, Billington and Baron-Cohen 2007), describes the bafflement of others who are unable 'to perceive words and numbers, colours, shapes and textures' (2006, p.2).

Nevertheless, as Wenn Lawson has suggested in the Foreword, experiencing synaesthesia can be disorientating for autistic children in the midst of the multiple sensory impacts that schools typically bring. Indeed, according to Jon, synaesthesia can also lead to ridicule if misunderstood:

▨ My own form of synaesthesia comes with numbers and letters, which is a bit more abstract. Blocks represented numbers, but this was totally confusing. For me, a 9 was less than 8. If you express this at school, people laugh, so you don't say it again. Colour was interesting – yellow made me feel nauseous. Green made me feel okay. (Jon)

Conclusion

The educational inclusion of autistic children cannot be separated from careful consideration of their sensory dispositions and needs, and no child should be feeling so overloaded and unwell that a day at school becomes something to be endured, tolerated and barely survived, possibly leading to some sort of 'meltdown' or shut down (Bogdashina 2016). Indeed, children who feel understood, relaxed and in control of their environment to the extent that they're not going to be forced to endure a sensory onslaught which might overwhelm them are potentially more able to tolerate the sights, sounds, smells and textures of a typical school day.

Key points

- A sensory response to the environment, and a need for sensory items, should not be confused with assessments of development and cognition. It should not be assumed that children who need physical items to support their learning are somehow delayed cognitively.

- Noise can be a highly exclusionary factor for autistic children and must be addressed in order to facilitate their learning and general well-being. However, it is not a question of volume levels alone.

- Schools need room, and different sorts of spaces, if they are to accommodate a diversity of learners. Outdoor spaces, if suitably managed, can be a vital resource.

- All pupils in a class might benefit from a quieter environment and less visual clutter.

- The sensory interests of autistic children may well be aligned with certain strengths that should be supported and encouraged.

Chapter 3

The Inclusion Delusion

Introduction

What do we mean by 'inclusion'? Inclusion into what? The school building? The classroom? The curriculum, pedagogy and extra-curricular activities in school? The hopes, dreams and expectations of other children? In fact, just as we saw, in Chapter 1, that 'autism' is much discussed but understood differently in various contexts, the same applies to the concept of inclusion, which continues to be a source of fierce debate and even acrimony, but without a common agreement of what it means (Imray and Colley 2017).

On the simplest level, educational inclusion refers to the placement of all children, regardless of their particular circumstances, dispositions or disabilities, within a mainstream school. It means they are within an ordinary, ideally local, school, rather than a special school, or one aimed at children who have been excluded from a number of other schools, such as a Pupil Referral Unit (PRU). Whether or not you agree with this as an ideal, as a broad brushstroke definition of inclusion – or at least integration (Lindsay 2007) – within an educational context, this is almost certainly what we all understand.

However, once we attempt to move beyond this simplistic description, all agreements and shared understandings seem to vanish, and are replaced instead by deliberations and discord, as well as, it must be said, a lot of unhappiness all round. Discussions about inclusion might take place from different standpoints, with debates at cross-purposes, from entrenched positionalities, which unsurprisingly make little headway. As Imray and Colley (2017, p.16) stated, the very meaning of inclusion remains elusive because for years on end, 'many of the travellers have been going round in circles'.

So in this chapter, I am going to try and tease out some of these issues and shed some new light on them, first, by summarising briefly the legal and historical background to inclusion. When all is said and done, what are the 'rights' of autistic children to educational inclusion and how do these rights fit in with their 'needs'? Are these concepts in some senses contradictory? In addition, and notwithstanding these rights, what are the problems of exclusion faced by autistic children, and what forms do they take?

I also explore the question of segregated schooling, and consider how ideas about inclusion have become confused with special school placement, attitudes and pedagogies. I reflect on how successful inclusion might be achieved, and argue that inclusion is, in fact, a matter for all children, not only for those designated with SEND.

Legal and historical background

Wherever you might stand on the inclusion spectrum, the legal and administrative framework for the educational inclusion of disabled children, both on an international and national level, is clear. The Salamanca Statement (UNESCO 1994), for example, is an international accord which reinforced the notion of educational inclusion, and was agreed by signatories in order 'to promote the approach of inclusive education, namely enabling schools to serve all children, particularly those with special educational needs' (1994, p.iii). This is backed up in legislation by the UN *Convention on the Rights of the Child* (UNCRC) (UNICEF 1989), which contains an affirmation of the right to primary education, secondary and higher education too, which should be 'accessible to all' (Article 28), and to prepare a child 'for responsible life in a free society' (Article 29) and 'the fullest possible social integration' (Article 23). This is important, because it means that the rights of disabled children to be educated and integrated into society are given the same weight as, for example, the right to life (Article 6), preservation of identity (Article 8) and protection from all forms of violence (Article 19), thus establishing a powerful basis on which to support and advocate for disabled children.

Later, the CRPD (UN DESA 2006) asserted the requirement for an 'inclusive education system at all levels', as the right to the availability of education is extended further to 'lifelong learning' (Article 24). Disabled children should be able to access education 'on an equal basis' along with other children in their communities, and this may only be realisable with the right 'accommodation', 'support measures', 'augmentative and alternative modes, means and formats of communication' (Article 24). Such measures might be a necessary means to enable 'persons with disabilities to participate effectively in a free society' where the ultimate goal is 'full inclusion' (Article 24). These provisions show us again that the receipt of an education is not considered to be an end in itself, but a conduit to societal integration. Therefore, educational inclusion, and the measures needed to obtain it, is seen as the lynchpin to participation and inclusion in society in the longer term.

As far as England is concerned, the Warnock Report (DES 1978) broadly promoted the concept of the education of children with special educational needs (SEN) in mainstream schools, and the *Education Act* (1981) provided that 'special educational provision' could now exist within an 'ordinary school', as long as certain conditions, such as 'the efficient use of resources', were met (Chapter 60). Since then, further legislation, such as the *Education Reform Act* (1988), the *Education Act* (1996) and the *Special Educational Needs and Disability Act (SENDA)* (2001), continued to reinforce the importance of educational inclusion for pupils with SEN.[1]

Later still, the *Equality Act* (2010) provided that a pupil must not be subject to exclusion, and confirmed that qualification bodies must 'minimise the extent to which disabled persons are disadvantaged in attaining the qualification because of their disabilities' (Part 6). Therefore, while the right of disabled children to be placed in mainstream school environments is further embedded over time, this is accompanied by additional provisions such as inclusion in the curriculum, being entered for exams and other issues of accessibility. More recently, the *Children and Families Act* (2014) established that Statements of SEN were to be replaced by Education, Health and Care (EHC) plans (Section 25). These may continue until the age of 25, and their overall purpose is to provide support for all aspects of the child or young person's life, including, for example, 'physical and

1   See www.educationengland.org.uk

mental health and emotional well-being', 'social and economic well-being' and 'the contribution made by them to society' (Section 25). Thus, the broader scope of inclusion, meaning more than simple physical placement in a mainstream school, is already entrenched in legislation, some of it several decades old.

Consequently, the various legal instruments and provisions show that over several decades, the rights of disabled children to receive an education on the same basis as all other children have gradually increased to encompass all aspects of physical, emotional and social life. Mainstream education, which must include access to the curriculum and exams, for example, is considered to be a conduit to longer-term social integration. Further, as we have seen, these provisions denote a gradual shift towards a sense that society, its systems and structures, need to adapt in order to include a greater diversity of individuals, constituting a powerful bedrock on which to base the rights to inclusion of disabled children. So why do the disagreements and difficulties continue?

Needs versus rights

One reason for this ongoing disharmony relates to what is arguably the most persistent debate in the field of SEND: the extent to which the education of disabled children is best served by an assertion of their 'rights', or alternatively, their 'needs'.

If a child is considered to have 'needs', this should signify that any difficulties are recognised and support is put in place. However, it can also mean that the child is potentially stigmatised, 'othered' and excluded from certain activities. Moreover, any problems the child is deemed to have are considered to stem from that child and their assessed disorder or difficulty (Terzi 2005). In other words, it is a 'within-child' model of disability, whereby factors associated with the environment, organisation, expectations and attitudes in school are not considered to be the source of a child's difficulties or inability to cope (Liasidou 2012).

The 'rights-based' perspective, however, suggests that we must set aside the idea that some children have 'needs', and focus instead on their right to a fully accessible and inclusive education (Sinclair Taylor 2000; Woronko and Killoran 2011) in which 'unique differences' are accommodated and integrated

(Lewis and Norwich 2005). According to Runswick-Cole and Hodge (2009), for example, the emphasis on the 'needs' of some children and the concomitant vocabulary of alienation is at the root of exclusionary practices. They argue for the replacement of the concept of 'special educational needs' with the notion of 'rights', asserting that in education 'children and young people are disabled through...being labelled as having "special needs"' (2009, p.199). Therefore, the notion of 'rights' places the responsibility on others to ensure that everything is in place to create an accessible educational environment for all children.

However, Allan (2008) has questioned whether legislation relating to inclusion and SEND has had a positive effect, and if it hasn't simply added to the 'confusion, frustration, guilt and exhaustion experienced by teachers' (2008, p.25). In addition, Lindsay (2007) considers that there is a lack of hard evidence that the growing emphasis on rights has led to good outcomes for children with SEND.

Meanwhile, others propose a middle ground. Ravet (2011), for example, suggests that the polarisation between 'needs' and 'rights' is unhelpful, and argues for an integrative position. She considers that 'labelling' can be exclusionary because it 'emphasises difference which can lead to marginalisation', but that it can also be 'inclusionary as it makes it possible to identify and meet individual needs' (2011, p.670). Furthermore, Liasidou (2012, p.13), who maintains that 'the linkage of inclusion with human rights should be urgently forged', warns of the potential dangers of undermining the rights of some children by dint of asserting the rights of others. In addition, models such as the 'capability approach' (Terzi 2005) situate the issue within a broader, more conceptual notion of 'justice' as a means to address this dilemma. It's a complex issue, especially as in the UK a child is unlikely to receive support unless they are considered to have 'needs' in the first instance.

The inclusion delusion

While these debates rumble on, the sad fact is that children with SEND are subject to high levels of exclusion. This is despite all of the legislation and policy documents outlined earlier, whether schools are supportive of the concept of inclusion or not, if teachers are in the 'needs' or 'rights' camp, or somewhere in between. And we mustn't forget that if autistic children are made to feel uncomfortable, overloaded and frustrated in school, this can lead to self-exclusion, whereby the child simply refuses to go to school at all (Goodall 2018).

> There was self-exclusion by me. By the 4th year my confidence was so knocked, I didn't want to join in. I would have stomach aches on a Sunday night. (Jon)

Nevertheless, on a simple – but devastating – level, exclusion tends to mean being ordered to be removed from the school, either temporarily or permanently. Dockrell, Peacey and Lunt (2002) found that children who had Statements of SEN were far more likely to be permanently excluded than pupils without Statements. Similarly, Jones *et al.* (2008) found that pupils with Statements of SEN were over three times more likely to be permanently excluded from school than the rest of the school population. And these exclusions are not always legal, as underscored by the Office of the Children's Commissioner in 2012:

> These are situations when a school requires a young person to leave the premises but does not record it as a formal exclusion. This might be for a fixed, usually short, period of time, or in the worst cases indefinitely. It also refers to instances when a young person or their family is 'persuaded' to move school, a move usually sold to the family and the child as an alternative to a permanent exclusion going on the child's record. (2012, p.16)

These actions, they maintain, are in contradiction of Article 28 of the UNCRC (UNICEF 1989), and argue that 'informal' or 'unofficial' exclusions are 'illegal regardless of whether they are done with the agreement of parents or carers' (Office of the Children's Commissioner 2012, p.58). Indeed, subsequent reports from the Office of the Children's Commissioner have continued to highlight this issue, as well as the problem of 'off-rolling', whereby pupils are removed from the school's register, often prior to GCSEs, but for reasons that cannot always be explained (Office of the Children's Commissioner 2017).

This situation appears to be particularly bad for autistic children (Batten *et al.* 2006; Humphrey 2008). For example, in a survey of 500 families run by the charity Ambitious About Autism (AAA), 23 per cent of parents reported that their autistic child had been formally excluded within the previous 12 months (AAA 2013). Later, in a survey of over 700 families, AAA found that 45 per cent of autistic children had been sent home illegally or denied a full education, and assert that autistic children are four times more likely to be permanently excluded from school than any other child (AAA 2016). How can we expect autistic children to achieve academically and develop their self-confidence and emotional well-being under these circumstances?

The parameters of exclusion

It's also important to understand that exclusion is a multi-faceted phenomenon that can be manifested in a range of ways; it doesn't just mean being excluded from the physical premises of the school. For example, some children can be barred from participation in extra-curricular activities (Jones 2002), from using certain equipment or from going on school trips (AAA 2016). Indeed, in my own study, hardly any of the 10 autistic children took part in after- or before-school clubs and activities, regardless of whether or not they wanted to. The main reason cited by school staff was that the children could not access these without support, and that the funding for TAs only covered the main school day.

■ I would like to join an art club at some point. (Grace, 14)

■ Choir is after school – I don't want to go. You have to go in a big group to a church. I'm afraid I might mess up if I do it. (Rose, 8)

■ I would like to do cross-country and football. (Zack, 10)

In addition, the SENCOs said that they asked the parents of the autistic children to come along on school trips, otherwise their child might not be able to take part. This was especially concerning because a number of the autistic children said that school trips were their favourite activities.

■ I always go on school trips unless there is a reason stopping me from going and my favourite was probably going to France in Year 6 because it was my first time going on a ferry, first time going to France and my first time being on a residential trip for more than three days. We did a lot of fun activities and I really enjoyed it. (Grace, 14)

This put the parents in quite a dilemma. Not only were they already unable to benefit from the social and work-related advantages of the extended school day, but they were also expected to devote some of their limited time to supporting their child on school trips. Therefore, exclusion of the child becomes a form of parental exclusion as well.

Not all of the children in my study attended school full-time, while others were excluded from certain subjects such as PE. In addition, even when technically present in school, all of the children, with the exception of one child, spent at least some time away from the rest of the main cohort, usually elsewhere on the school premises. Sometimes they were taken out of lessons part way through, and were expected to catch up on their return, even though they had less time to complete the task and had only received a partial explanation of the activity. Furthermore, the autistic children were usually on their own with a TA, in a small group in the class or elsewhere in the school, meaning that they had limited input from the class teacher. This is significant because research shows that the class teacher is the lynchpin to successful inclusion of autistic pupils and those with SEND (Humphrey and Symes 2011).

One child in my study was educated separately from the other children, but within the same classroom, at a workstation. No doubt the well-intentioned teacher felt that this was a way of achieving inclusion, especially given the limitations of space, discussed in the previous chapter. However, as a method of inclusion, this did not seem especially satisfactory either, as this child was regularly distracted by the activities of the rest of the class. This made it difficult for him to concentrate and learn, especially as he appeared to have a number of sensory issues. Such an arrangement also ran the risk of stigmatising him from the point of view of the rest of the class.

■ In Year 4, I was basically put in a 'cupboard' – a store room which was emptied to become a classroom for me – with 1-1 support. (George)

■ I did something called 'Talking Time' – it's a fun activity – I'm the only one in the class who does it. Maybe I'm special. I miss some of my favourite lessons sometimes. But some of the lessons are boring and so it's okay to miss those. (Rose, 8)

Certainly, the school staff felt this sort of within-school segregation was necessary, and cited speech and language therapy and sensory input, an inability to access the class activity, and working on social or life skills as the main reasons. Meanwhile, some children spent time off the school premises altogether in order to access therapy, for example.

However, despite the rationale for this segregation, there was no evident mechanism in place to enable the autistic children to catch up on work missed, even when they were absent for entire sections of the curriculum on a regular basis. Furthermore, in some cases, withdrawal from class seemed almost arbitrary and to be done on a whim of the TA, who would take the opportunity to catch up on paperwork, especially as, unlike the teachers, they do not have paid administration and preparation time.

Therefore, it's important to realise that exclusion does not simply mean being expulsed from a school, and that many mini-exclusions, both within-school and within-class, are operating for autistic children in our education system. A child who is 'included' in a mainstream school might still be spending part of their week at home, or not take part in clubs or trips, or spend little time with their classmates. Or a child might even be in the same physical environment as the other children, but seated apart, with a TA. And so, even though being able to withdraw or complete alternative activities may, in some circumstances, be beneficial to the child, this is by no means always the case. It's important that the advantages to the child of these arrangements are clearly identified, rather than this being a 'go to' approach for educational inclusion when in reality, it is nothing of the sort.

Are some strategies for inclusion a form of exclusion in disguise? If, as we saw earlier in this chapter, educational inclusion is considered a necessary conduit to fuller social integration in the longer term, the same principle applies to exclusion too. Being excluded from school is harmful and can damage the life chances of any child, as summarised by Thomas (2012, p.480):

> This is in the damage done to individuals' sense of worth and identity where they see themselves, through major differences between themselves and their peers, conspicuously excluded from the expectations, the activities, the resources, the worlds of those peers.

Segregated schooling

Let us now turn to the question of segregated schooling. By this I mean placement in special school or some sort of alternative provision such as a PRU or a resource base attached to a mainstream school. Given the difficulties I have described, could it be the case that autistic children are better served by some form of segregated schooling, especially as, in some accounts, they are presented as disruptive, alien presences, unable to fit into a mainstream educational system that 'cannot be altered' to accommodate them (Glashan, Mackay and Grieve 2004, p.56)? Indeed, Jones (2002) and Jones et al. (2008) assert that 'inclusion' as a concept applies just as much to special education as mainstream settings, while Lindsay (2007, p.18) hints at a similar position, questioning whether inclusion should only be conceived of as meaning 'full-time education in a mainstream class'.

In fact, some commentators simply reject the notion of mainstream inclusion outright for at least some disabled children, and autistic children in particular. In the Foreword to Cigman (2007, p.x), for example, in a reversal of her previous position (DES 1978), Warnock criticises 'the British Council for Disabled People... who regard inclusion in mainstream schools as something to which disabled children are entitled to as of right', a rather concerning attitude given, as we have seen, it is indeed their 'right'. Meanwhile Cigman (2007, p.xix), in the Editorial introduction, argues against those she describes as 'radical inclusionists'. For Cigman (2007, p.xxiv), autistic children constitute 'a group of children for whom the benefits of mainstream education are widely viewed with scepticism', while in the same book, Wing (2007, p.28) similarly criticises 'the theories of idealists who have no knowledge of or empathy for children with autism' by seeking to place them in a mainstream school. Wing (2007, p.32) considers that special school placements are more suitable for 'many, though not all' autistic children.

However, for Liasidou (2012), special schools do not provide the answer, as they are somewhat spuriously justified on the basis that they can better meet the needs of some children, thus 'leaving intact the normal operation of mainstream schooling' (2012, p.22). Having ejected a child from a mainstream setting, schools can just carry on as before, consciences salved by the notion that a special school can do the job. Indeed, for Sinclair Taylor (2000), the tenets of the UNCRC (UNICEF 1989) cannot be achieved within a system of 'normal and non-normal schooling' (2000, p.28), a point also echoed in Runswick-Cole and Hodge (2009). Furthermore, when we think of 'exclusion', we tend to associate this with 'exclusion from' a mainstream setting. In fact, according to figures from the DfE (2017c), the rate of fixed-period exclusions of pupils in special schools is higher than for state primary and secondary schools.

Notwithstanding these points, there is no doubt that some special school placements can work well for autistic children, as my contributor George found when he transferred from a mainstream primary school to a special school:

■ It was completely different at the special school – the exact opposite, the staff were great, I had no exclusions whatsoever, everything was great. (George)

Another option, as many readers will be aware, is to have a resource base attached to a mainstream school. Hesmondhalgh and Breakey (2001) and Hesmondhalgh (2006), for example, describe the benefits not only of a modified curriculum for autistic children of secondary school age, but also of a specifically designed resource base. However, Liasidou (2012) considers that resource units are inherently exclusionary, as they are 'mini special schools', which do not, in practice, enable pupils to integrate into the mainstream:

> These units are starkly oriented to a segregating model, and seldom do they function as a transitional mode of education, aimed at facilitating the gradual inclusion of disabled children in mainstream classes. (2012, p.25)

Moreover, Lloyd-Smith and Tarr (2000), citing Sinclair Taylor (1995), suggest that pupils' perceptions of the value of being placed in a resource base might be at variance with those of the school staff and associated professionals:

> ...the pupils experienced the unit as excluding and marginalizing, not inclusive as professionals in the school and local authority believed it to be. (2000, p.61)

And so, however problematic mainstream inclusion might be for autistic children, segregated schooling cannot be assumed to provide the answer either.

■ The fact that we have 'a system' is problematic, so inflexible, so geared to an imagined child. Autistic kids need to be supported as autistic kids, recognising that everyone's normal is different. Play, learning, friendships, all aspects of school, seem to be only recognised as significant if we fit into some weird standardised 'normal'. I think this is an issue for many kids, not just autistic ones. (Kabie)

Inclusion: a sub-section of special education

Given the view of some commentators that many autistic children would fare better in special schools, it is perhaps unsurprising that the very meaning of inclusion has become conflated with special education. According to Liasidou (2012), for example, 'inclusion' as a concept has come to denote little more than a sub-section of special education, where 'several disguised forms of marginalization, discrimination and exclusion are operating' (2012, p.9). Indeed, for Liasidou (2012, p.21), inclusive education has been reduced to a 'special education artefact' where the focus is on certain children, namely, those with disabilities, low attainment or behavioural issues. Liasidou (2012) expresses a particular concern that as a result of this conflation of inclusion with special education, schools can play the system whereby they 'discreetly marginalize and exclude certain students and prevent them from adding negative value to a school's performance indicators' (2012, p.20).

Further, according to Slee and Allan (2001), too many of the methods, philosophies and approaches of special education have been used in the name of inclusion, a concept which can be misappropriated to reinforce 'unreconstructed notions of schooling and educational defectiveness' (2001, p.174). Similarly, for Thomas (2012, p.475), inclusive education is considered to be a matter for certain children only: it is 'still like an island, considered as a separate territory from mainstream education, with its own discourses, policies and practices'. In fact, we tend to assume that by 'inclusion' we mean 'inclusion of' children with SEND, which, of course, immediately raises the possibility that they might not be 'included', showing how even by talking about 'inclusion' we are already thinking about 'exclusion'. In these ways, the notion of inclusion has become a contranym, a word employed to denote the opposite of itself.

Successful inclusion

As we have seen, the association of 'inclusion' with 'special educational needs' seems to sow the seeds for exclusionary attitudes and practices, whereby some children are deemed to be 'other', and so liable to be ejected from seemingly welcoming and inclusive spaces. Therefore, let us now consider what successful inclusion might look like, both as a concept and in practice.

To start with, simple placement in a mainstream setting is not 'inclusion' but 'integration'. The distinction is an important one, because if the latter 'suggests simply relocating students into unchanged educational systems', the former 'suggests a radical re-organization of schools in order to meet the diversity of learner needs' (Liasidou 2012, p.9). And so, as a core principle, inclusion must necessitate some sort of change or adaptation – at the very least – to accommodate a diversity of learners.

Inclusion in a mainstream school may therefore necessitate adjustments to the physical environment of the school, but also teaching styles and the curriculum (Jones *et al.* 2008; Norwich and Kelly 2004). Indeed, Jordan (2005) makes the case for 'an inclusive curriculum', arguing that curriculum planning must contain at the earliest stage the potential to include a diversity of learners. This is a concept evocative of the principles of the 'universal design for learning' espoused by the CRPD (UN DESA 2006), also advocated by Woronko and Killoran (2011) and Liasidou (2012).

Inclusive education should also extend further to relationships with other pupils, both within and outside school, as well as school staff (Jones *et al.* 2008). Therefore, to be included in school necessitates social acceptance and participation (Norwich and Kelly 2004), as well as being able to attend after-school clubs (Jones *et al.* 2008).

And so, inclusion, if it is to be meaningful, must incorporate the curriculum, extra-curricular activities and design of the school building from the earliest planning stages. It's also about social relationships and that intangible phenomenon – attitudes – and having the same expectations for autistic children as for any others (Thomas 2012). Such an approach is ultimately much more likely to succeed than trying to achieve the inclusion of disabled children after the fact, by bolting on adaptations and accommodations once all the core structures and programmes are in place.

It means that everyone is able to get on and learn and enjoy themselves without running into problems. And, of course, there's going to be little problems that pop up – that's part of life – but for them to be small ones. (George)

■ It's about instilling confidence in the child, confidence in who they are and their ability, not for it to be pointed out that they cannot do things; it should be pointed out that they can do other things. There needs to be *appropriate* support which is sought from or with the guidance of actually autistic people. (Jon)

Moreover, it's important to understand that inclusion and exclusion are not fixed entities, and that what might be exclusionary for one child can be inclusionary for another. For example, it was evident in my study that in some circumstances, spending time away from the main cohort was of clear benefit to some children. Indeed, Norwich and Kelly (2004, p.62) consider that 'full-time mainstream class placement' is contrary to the notion of 'inclusive schooling'. And I certainly found that time away from the class could provide an opportunity for the autistic children to take a break from the noise and the crowded classroom, speak confidentially to a TA or focus on activities of interest. One autistic child enjoyed the small group sessions he sometimes participated in, and viewed these other children to be his friends. Therefore, it is possible to state, somewhat cautiously, that withdrawal from class – especially self-withdrawal – can be beneficial as a method of inclusion. However, this is not to be confused with the arbitrary removal of a child from certain activities, or the failure to make the curriculum accessible. Nor is this the same as school refusal, which is a different matter entirely.

Inclusion: a matter for all

In the various ways discussed so far in this chapter, exclusion emerges as a potentially widespread phenomenon, multi-faceted in its manifestations and entrenched in a complex relationship with inclusion (Allan 2010). We have also seen that inclusion extends well beyond simple placement in a mainstream school, to incorporate the curriculum, trips and clubs, relationships and the environment, for example. Crucially, these phenomena are not fixed, and what works for one autistic child might not work for another.

Inclusion is also about equality of opportunities: for all children to be able to learn, progress and participate in school, in the fullest sense. It is about having the same expectations for all children, not positioning some as problems to be resolved or as disruptive presences upsetting the status quo.

> The class teacher – she didn't seem to get the problem whatsoever. I remember there being one morning when I couldn't stand in line for whatever reason. I just couldn't stand in line, I don't know why, but she thought I was just being a naughty child. (George)

Indeed, according to the autistic adults in my study, inclusion derives much more from an acceptance of diversity and recognition that all children, in some senses, have 'needs', rather than targeting some with a raft of inclusion strategies, which might serve paradoxically to exclude them further. Similarly, Thomas (2012, p.486) argues the following:

> The future contribution of inclusive education hinges on its ability to retreat from histories of identify-assess-diagnose-help and to examine the ways in which schools enable community and encourage students' belief in themselves as members of such community.

Therefore, inclusion is a matter for all children, not just those with the label of 'special educational needs', and all children can benefit from well thought-out inclusive practices (Hehir *et al.* 2016). As Lenehan (2017) stated, in a report that focuses predominantly on the health of autistic children and those with learning disabilities:

> These children are part of our community, not external to it. They are our nieces and nephews, the children of our neighbours and friends. In a very real way they are our children too. We have a responsibility as a community to do the best for these children, to support them in the best possible way in order to allow them to thrive. (2017, p.4)

Conclusion

As we have seen, the concept of inclusion continues to create discord and confusion, with little shared understanding of what it looks like or how it should operate. This is despite significant administrative and legislative backup promoting educational inclusion, both nationally and internationally. Indeed, debates continue about whether there should be an emphasis on the 'rights' of pupils with SEND as opposed to their 'needs', without either, it seems to me, being satisfactorily met. And whatever your view on this, it appears unavoidable within the UK context that assessment and identification of 'needs' is necessary in order to obtain those very rights to which all children are entitled. To put it very simply, unless children are considered to have named problems or difficulties of some sort, they are unlikely to obtain the necessary support that legislation has prescribed.

My study also indicates that on the whole, inclusion appears to be operating in a rather fractured and unsatisfactory way, with the presence of autistic children in mainstream schools still contested. An autistic child might be perceived as a disruptive, alien presence, who belongs to someone – and somewhere – else. And so some autistic children face outright exclusion from school, while others are subject to part-time timetables, alternative curricula and exclusion from clubs and trips, but without any consistent justification or consideration of the broader educational, social and psychological implications. Too often inclusion is perceived as a facet of special education; however, the philosophies, approaches and methodologies of special schools cannot, by their very nature, further inclusion in mainstream settings.

While it was certainly the case that small group work, withdrawal from class and even alternative learning targets could be beneficial for some of the children, on the whole it was these very strategies for inclusion that formed the driver for exclusion of the children in my cohort. Indeed, because of these issues, the very meaning of inclusion itself is in danger of denoting little more than being physically present within a mainstream school (Humphrey 2008; Norwich 2014), rather than overcoming barriers and creating equality of access (Rioux and Valentine 2006).

Therefore, while it is clear that there is no fixed formula or model for inclusion, and that different schools – and especially, different children – will benefit from a variety of arrangements, certain helpful principles can be usefully applied. Crucially, the well-being of the child should always dictate specific educational arrangements, with decisions reached holistically, incorporating the views of the parents and the child, and should never be made on the basis of a label alone. Indeed, it is not necessarily the action itself that defines whether or not it is exclusionary or inclusive, but how the decision is reached, and if it is genuinely beneficial to the child.

> To be able to go to my local school and not have to travel a long distance or live away from home to receive an education. To be treated with respect as a fully whole autistic person rather than a broken non-autistic person. To be enabled to create a positive self-identity. To be able to learn at my own pace: to be offered the same opportunities in life: an education tailored to my needs, utilising my strengths and finding ways to overcome my difficulties. It doesn't mean doing exactly the same as everyone else, but it does mean being treated with respect and teachers understanding me enough to teach me in an appropriate way. (Kabie)

If inclusion does not mean everyone doing the same things, in the same ways, at the same time, neither does it mean a pick-and-mix approach where inclusion is only partial and conditional on certain criteria being met. Indeed, if all children are perceived as equal members of a school community with the right to the same expectations and opportunities, this doesn't cancel out any support needs some individuals might have. Ultimately, inclusion concerns all children, not just those who are 'special'.

Key points

- Whatever the views of individual practitioners and researchers, the legal rights to educational inclusion for autistic children are long-standing and formidable.

- Notwithstanding the disadvantages of identifying some children as having 'needs', this is often the only conduit to obtaining suitable support.

- Making the assumption that autistic children might be better placed in a special school can be a way of simply denying responsibility for those children; special schools also exclude children.

- Exclusion can take many forms. Some inclusionary practices can, in fact, be exclusionary.

- How inclusion operates can vary greatly according to the particular circumstances, ethos and attitudes of staff within individual schools. Decisions about individual children should not be made on the basis of a label alone, and should include parents and children too.

- Inclusion is a matter for all children in a school, not for a few with a label of SEND. A school is a community, and all children should be seen as equal members of that community.

Chapter 4

Educational Priorities

Introduction

In the last chapter, we saw how autistic children in mainstream schools can be subject to partial timetables, or a schedule which is interrupted for the sake of interventions, or even entirely different in major parts to that of other children. These approaches are carried out in the name of inclusion, and while they might work under certain circumstances, they can also be a form of exclusion in disguise.

So all of this raises the question of what autistic children should be learning in school. The same as everyone else? Largely the same, but with a few extras? Is it more important to focus on socialisation, communication and 'life skills' rather than the academic subjects? In an already crowded curriculum with, as I found in my own study, schools expected to carry a range of academic, social and affective roles, what gets dropped? And importantly, who makes these decisions and what measures are used to evaluate progress in any alternative areas? Indeed, given that data from the DfE regularly show that autistic children[1] fare poorly in school tests and exams, it's important to consider the extent to which this might result, at least in part, from exclusion from certain subjects or from the main teaching programme.

In addition, attitudes vary on whether or not autistic children should even be doing tests and exams, with some adults in my study, for example, expressing concerns that they might be too

---

1   Data collected by the DfE on children with 'ASD by primary need', with a Statement of SEN, on School Action Plus (generally before 2015), or with an EHC plan or on SEN support.

stressful and difficult for autistic children to tackle (Douglas *et al.* 2012). Indeed, the same DfE data sources also indicate that in some areas, autistic children might not even be taking tests at all.

And so in this chapter I consider the question of educational priorities and explore the different facets of this debate in a little more detail. I discuss the implications of a modified curriculum and focus in particular on the value of an academic curriculum compared with a programme targeting social and life skills for autistic children. I also explore some of the issues relating to tests and exams, and explain how the question of educational priorities must always be linked to ideas about outcomes. You will see that my research showed some interesting divergences of perspectives between different participants on these issues, a point that underscores the importance of giving this whole matter the time, thought and reflection it requires.

Fixed versus modified curriculum

It's not unusual to come across the view that a fixed and inflexible curriculum is entirely unhelpful for autistic children. According to Emam and Farrell (2009, p.414), for example, teachers of autistic pupils feel 'completely trapped by the constraints of the national curriculum', while Whitaker (2007, p.170) asserts that autistic children 'require the explicit teaching of skills and understanding which are not part of the conventional academic curriculum'. For Hesmondhalgh and Breakey (2001, p.142), lessons for autistic children 'must take the pupil into areas s/he would be denied if it were left to the national curriculum', which in itself cannot provide the 'something more' that such pupils require (2001, p.115). Liasidou (2012, p.34) has also argued that 'socially just pedagogies entail diversifying and changing the curriculum...in order to meet learner diversity'. And so, according to some commentators, a fixed curriculum, such as a national curriculum, can be limiting and unhelpful for autistic children.

However, Jones (2002) is of the view that the national curriculum can in fact be adapted for autistic children, while Douglas *et al.* (2012) avoided considering alternative curricula in their report on assessment for pupils with SEND precisely because of their association with 'exclusion from a mainstream curriculum' (2012, p.33).

> I think they should do the same curriculum. Especially in primary school, you're learning the basics of everything, so it is very important. If they're not doing the same curriculum, it would be an obvious red flag to the other children that there is something different about that child. They'd be thinking – why is that person different? (George)

Therefore, rather than potentially stigmatising some children with an adapted or even alternative schedule, as my contributor George has highlighted, it would be preferable to try to devise a curriculum that is inherently more inclusive in the first instance (Jordan 2005).

Interestingly, the parents in my study were more likely to recommend an alternative, adapted or partial curriculum compared with the autistic adults (some of whom were parents themselves, although this was not a feature of my study). Five parents said they would be prepared for certain subjects to be dropped so that their child could focus on other skills such as communication, social skills and therapeutic input, as well as subjects or activities that particularly interested them. Nevertheless, they were unclear about which subjects should be set aside in order to make room for these alternative activities, although Geography, German and PE were suggested at different times.

Academic versus social or life skills

Which are more important for autistic children in schools: academic achievement or social and life skills? Parsons *et al.* (2011), for example, found that as well as academic attainment, other goals were considered to be equally important for autistic children, including social understanding, physical and emotional well-being and independence skills:

> Many children on the autism spectrum can achieve a high level of academic success, but without the necessary skills and understandings in other areas of their life, may fail to benefit from

these in terms of their future education, employment or living arrangements. (Parsons *et al.* 2011, p.59)

And so, according to these ideas, academically able autistic children might be unable to reap the rewards of academic attainment in later life if they do not possess the social skills they also require. Similarly, Dockrell *et al.* (2012) found that parents of autistic children were more likely to prioritise social outcomes and friendships, while Harvey (2011), who asked school staff and parents what the educational priorities should be for autistic children, found that for both groups 'academic learning was the least important outcome… and social skills was the most important' (2011, p.114). Therefore, certain curriculum subjects might be dropped so that autistic children can be taught these additional skills in school. Indeed, according to some of the school staff in my own research, learning independence and acquiring life skills were the reasons why some of the autistic children had a modified curriculum.

However, when Wittemeyer *et al.* (2011b) interviewed autistic adults on this issue, 58 per cent of respondents said that they had not achieved the qualifications they wanted at school, hinting at a greater value placed on academic achievement than some research might suggest. Wittemeyer *et al.* (2011b) also found that studies into assessment and outcomes for autistic students focused on 'functional goals' (2011b, p.38), and that 'academic attainment did not feature' (2011b, p.37). This points to an important issue in the education of autistic children: the fact that scholastic achievement might fade from view if the focus shifts instead on to social and life skills.

■ English and Maths are important, but I think that the subjects you really enjoy and want to use in your future are equally as important. For me, Art and ICT are the most important, even more so than Maths and English. (Grace, 14)

■ Educational priorities should be about encouraging children to learn and increase their potential in life and to help them into a career they will excel in. I don't see these as being any different for children that aren't autistic. (Michael)

In my own study, the 10 parents of autistic children and 10 autistic adults were asked about the educational priorities for their children, for autistic children in particular, and for all children in primary schools in general. In the event, there were some revealing similarities and divergences between the parents and the autistic adults. For example, approximately half of the autistic adults and half of the parents felt that happiness and well-being were the most important priorities in school, showing the greatest area of similarity between both groups. Moreover – and bearing in mind that some school staff highlighted this as justifying a modified curriculum – independence and life skills were not asserted by many in either group as an area of particular priority in the primary school phase.

However, the parents stressed the importance of social skills more than any other educational priority, as had the parents in the study from Dockrell *et al.* (2012), for example. Meanwhile, the autistic adults emphasised academic skills more than any other educational priority, showing the main differences between the two groups. This is perhaps significant because again, as was implied in Wittemeyer *et al.* (2011b), the academic skills of autistic children and adults are shown to matter, *to them*.

Nevertheless, despite the fact that most of the autistic adults did not emphasise socialisation as a specific educational priority, other comments and anecdotes in the broader interviews highlighted the significant social difficulties some of them had experienced in school (see Chapter 9 for a further discussion on this). Importantly, though, this did not mean that academic skills were somehow unimportant as a result.

In addition, as well as underscoring the importance of the core curriculum, the autistic adults also tended to refer to more fundamental issues, such as engendering an enthusiasm for learning, nurturing talent and individual characteristics, and helping to develop a sense of self-esteem, a view also shared by some of the parents. Therefore, while parents might emphasise socialisation for their autistic children, it's worth looking at what might fuel these attitudes, and to consider that what really matters is their child's happiness, and their perception of how this might be achieved. In short, many of the parents felt that friendships were the lynchpin to their child's happiness and educational inclusion, so it is unsurprising that socialisation was a key priority for them.

> Rounded education yes – but targeting their interests. Need to be thinking about it at a young age – doing something you're good at and which is useful, is joy to an autistic person. I was continually told off because I wanted to do more specialist things. (Jon)

> I think reading, writing and being comfortable with yourself are the important things. Learning about ourselves and learning how to be happy, how to get by in life, how to develop a positive sense of self and how to get our needs met. (Kabie)

Tests and exams

Testing in schools tends to get a bad press, particularly in the primary phase of education, where there is a perception that there are too many tests, and that they are of limited value for the children themselves. The parents involved in my own study revealed mixed feelings about the value of tests and exams for their children, as did school staff. Similarly, the autistic adult participants expressed a range of views about this issue, but also emphasised the importance of an individualised approach, taking into account the social ramifications of tests, for example. As far as the autistic children were concerned, some of them valued and enjoyed tests, while others disliked them:

I do believe that testing youngsters of a young age against the national average is pointless for the student and it's only to benefit the staff and the schools. The value is to see if children are on track, what they are good at, what they are not good at, so they can see where they need to put more focus. (George)

Tests and exams are important to gauge a child's skill level in a subject. Excessive testing, or studying exclusively to pass tests, are, of course, counterproductive. (Michael)

Whatever your own view on this, it is an unavoidable fact that if children are excluded from the whole or aspects of the main curriculum, such as being regularly sent out of class for social interventions, then they cannot be meaningfully assessed in the areas they have missed or in subjects that have been set aside. Indeed, when I looked into DfE data, I found that autistic children (as defined by the DfE – see footnote 1 at the start of this chapter) were either not performing very well in school tests and exams or, in the case of Phonics in particular, were often not even being assessed. We must consider, therefore, the extent to which this phenomenon is due to the lack of ability of autistic children, or simply the fact that they are missing lessons in school (let alone, as we saw in the last chapter, being temporarily or permanently excluded from school).

Furthermore, according to some accounts, pupils with SEND are considered to impact negatively on school performance figures, which has resulted in a significant problem of 'off-rolling' (Office of the Children's Commissioner 2017). Dockrell *et al.* (2002), for example, suggest that schools struggle to be effective both in terms of 'high attainments' and 'inclusive' when they have high numbers of pupils with SEND, with the result that some children are excluded from assessments. Sinclair Taylor (2000) is also of the view that children are being excluded from school as a result of the introduction of league tables and the resulting pressure on schools to present a good picture of themselves academically. Indeed, according to Lindsay (2007), some studies show that there is a negative correlation between inclusion and overall school attainment, to the extent that the schools with fewer children with SEND fare better overall. So are autistic pupils being excluded from tests and exams because of concerns about school performance figures? Are they deemed to be of low ability and thus a threat to the academic reputation of the school?

In fact, the *Code of Practice* (DfE 2015a, p.94) urges teachers to 'set targets which are deliberately ambitious' for pupils with SEND, underscoring the point that all pupils deserve – in the broadest sense – high expectations. In this same document there is also a relatively strong emphasis on qualifications, asserting that young people with SEND should be taking 'rigorous, substantial' qualifications which are 'nationally recognised' for apprenticeships and internships, for example (DfE 2015a, pp.130–131). And so there is little excuse or justification for assuming that autistic children don't merit qualifications, just as other children do. Moreover, Dyson and Farrell (2007) assert that statistics showing low attainment for schools with high levels of pupils with SEND should be treated with caution, stating that they were unable to find 'any convincing evidence that inclusion...has any meaningful negative impact on overall levels of attainment in schools' (2007, p.124).

This raises a further question about autistic children and school tests: are they accessible in the first instance? In my own study, for example, I found that there were some significant issues regarding access to tests, with participants providing a whole raft of reasons why autistic children might not be able to take part in them. These included the nature and format of the tests themselves, the particular dispositions of the autistic children, and the circumstances under which they might be taken (Wood 2017).

A number of participants considered that the wording of tests can be confusing for autistic children, or that they are too long. Other participants commented on the problems caused by a change of routine when tests and exams take place, while some considered not only that autistic children might lack the intrinsic motivation to do tests, but that they also find the whole process stressful. According to the TAs, the autistic children could also get 'stuck' on a question they couldn't answer and would be unable to simply leave it out and move on. Some of the autistic adults also referred to the problems of public exposure, such as when marks are read out loud in class. This applied even if they had done well, they said.

> I hate having other people read my work. Some teachers have us do peer assessment and mark our partner's test/writing instead of our own or the teacher marking it. (Grace, 14)

Therefore, alongside all of the other problems relating to curriculum access that autistic children might face, it could well be the case that for some, at least, tests and exams are also difficult to access. For example, Jones *et al.* (2011), in the context of the inclusion of autistic children in mainstream schools, emphasise the importance of 'equality of access' (2011, p.26) for tests and exams. Similarly, Wittemeyer *et al.* (2011a) consider that staff must be able to demonstrate 'a good understanding of the framework for access arrangements for exams' (2011a, p.40) if autistic children are to be suitably included in school. And so it seems evident that ideas about inclusion should extend not only to the curriculum, but to tests as well.

In fact, in England, a plethora of access arrangements for tests and exams is available (STA 2017), and although none are specific to autistic children, they should certainly help (Wood 2016). Indeed, Cox *et al.* (2006), in a study based in the USA, found not only that there was a correlation between accommodations for tests and the participation of students with disabilities in those tests, but that there was also a corresponding reduction in school exclusions. Similarly, Feldman, Kim and Elliott (2011) consider that accommodations in tests for students with learning disabilities improve their test-related self-efficacy and motivation. Moreover, it's worth noting that a key criterion in terms of eligibility for access arrangements in England is that these accommodations must 'reflect normal classroom practice' (STA 2017, p.5), meaning that if autistic children do not receive the support they need in class, they might be additionally disadvantaged when it comes to tests and exams too. Unfortunately, the school staff in my own study were largely unaware of the range of access arrangements already available for pupils with SEND (STA 2017), and so they were not taken advantage of to any great extent. Indeed, some feared 'over-helping', considered a far worse crime than not providing the accommodations autistic children might be entitled to.

So at the very least, autistic children should be helped to participate in tests and exams with the support of the access arrangements to which they are entitled. Moreover, Lazarus *et al.* (2009) found that the application of the principle of 'universal assessment' reduces the need for access arrangements in the first place. Similarly, Douglas *et al.* (2012, p.4) consider that assessment procedures 'should be designed to include the diverse range of children and young people within the educational system'. In other words, well-designed tests and exams should reduce the need for access arrangements for certain children. And all children, regardless of their categorisation of SEND, should be included in local and national assessment schemes if possible.

An additional issue concerns the extent to which autistic children might interpret and respond to certain questions and demonstrate their understanding. This might mean that they are getting the answers right, but have interpreted the question differently from the person who set the paper, as my contributor Michael has so eloquently expressed below. However, these differences are not always accounted for in current assessment processes and mark schemes. This suggests the need for a more radical shift in how tests and exams are written, designed and marked in order to be genuinely inclusive for autistic children and adults.

The current education system needs a massive overhaul as it is wholly unsuitable for any child that doesn't fit the government's pre-disposed criteria for how children should be. Children are tested excessively, trained to pass tests instead of encouraging flexibility of thinking, and this particularly affects autistic children who often take a different approach, yet regularly get the answers correct. This actually disadvantages the out-of-the-box thinking autistic children often have, as teachers want to see the answers achieved in their way. (Michael)

Outcomes

The question of educational priorities is inevitably linked to that of outcomes. To set a curriculum for a child is unavoidably to make choices about what is important for that child, both in the here and now, and in the future. And so it's not a decision to be taken lightly.

Jones (2002, p.114), for example, considers that staff 'working with pupils with ASDs need to take a long-term perspective and work on skills needed in adult life during the school years'. Similarly, both Douglas *et al.* (2012) and Wittemeyer *et al.* (2011b) are of the view that assessment, in order to be meaningful, must also be linked to the question of outcomes. Indeed, according to Douglas *et al.* (2012), there is too much emphasis on 'inputs' for children with SEND and not enough on outcomes, and Jones *et al.* (2008) underscore the importance of defining and planning good outcomes, particularly in relation to different types of academic provision.

This again raises the issues of what to measure, and how. For Dockrell *et al.* (2002, p.41), the 'assessment of educational outcomes is fraught with technical problems', and Parsons *et al.* (2011) found a lack of coherence and consensus on which outcomes should be measured for interventions or educational provision for autistic children. Dockrell *et al.* (2002) suggest the four possible measures that can be used to evaluate academic provision are those relating to 'academic, effective, social' and 'life chance', and that gauges of outcomes might include measures of self-esteem and friendship-making, as well as educational attainment.

Meanwhile, Douglas *et al.* (2012) are of the view that although school tests should be designed to accommodate a diversity of pupils, progress ought still to be recorded in additional areas for children with SEND. Grouping studies into the four broad categories of attainment, attendance, happiness and independence-related outcomes, they assert that assessments could include 'more specific outcomes such as resilience, self-esteem, well-being, relationship building, optimism, employment, independent living skills and successful transition after school' (Douglas *et al.* 2012, p.6). However, as laudable as these aims are, the mechanisms by which they could be measured would inevitably be both complex and subjective. How would a teacher decide if a child was optimistic, for example?

Furthermore, while these controversies rage, most accounts provide a negative picture of the longer-term outcomes of autistic children and adults. The charity AAA highlighted that less than one in four autistic young people continue their education beyond school, and that young people with a statement of SEN at the age of 16 are twice as likely to not be in education, employment or training (NEET) as young people without SEN (AAA 2012). In addition, in the CRPD (UN DESA 2006), it is asserted that 'persons with disabilities are disproportionally affected by poverty and overrepresented among the poorest in the world' (Article 29), and Dockrell *et al.* (2002, p.46) affirm that the 'single most likely destination for many disabled people appears to be poverty'. For Wittemeyer *et al.* (2011b, p.48), school exclusion is a crucial factor in this area, citing an interviewee who asserted that 'being permanently excluded from school is one of the main drivers of poor outcomes for any child'. From these texts, therefore, a powerful chronicle emerges of poor life chances for autistic people, suggesting an urgent need to increase their access to education, qualifications and opportunities.

■ It should be about instilling confidence in themselves, not taking it away. Autistic people find it very difficult to get a job. (Jon)

In my own study, the autistic children expressed a range of ambitions for the future, but this was not often acknowledged by school staff or factored into their educational programmes. Instead, I found that curriculum decisions for the autistic children were sometimes set according to a generalised notion of autism as a condition beset by social interaction, communication and sensory impairments, with little consideration of the longer-term impact of these arrangements on their educational attainment. Indeed, missing parts of the core curriculum was considered unimportant compared with the ostensible drive towards independence and life skills, but with little real sense of how progress in these areas might be measured. However, some of the parents and autistic adult participants emphasised the importance of enabling the autistic children to develop their interests in school, an important issue that will be discussed in the next chapter.

Conclusion

Deciding on a curriculum for a child – especially if it is to be different from that of the rest of the class – is a complex issue and, as we have seen, there are no easy answers. Indeed, in this chapter, I have deliberately avoided drawing any firm conclusions on what the educational priorities of autistic children *should* be, precisely because it is so important to adopt an individualised approach. What seems clear, however, is that to exclude a child from the curriculum and activities of the other children is to create limitations and barriers to the child's progress and future development, as well as to potentially stigmatise that child.

Therefore, whatever your view on this issue, it seems at the very least that an adapted or alternative curriculum should not be assumed to be the right formula for an autistic child in school, and that educators must consider carefully the implications of such a decision. Removing part of the curriculum for any child is, in fact, quite a major decision to make, and should only be done after all efforts have been made to provide a fully inclusive timetable.

Furthermore, although we do not know the extent to which poor performance in national assessments as shown in the DfE data can be explained by the problems of curriculum exclusion that autistic children face, it is perhaps self-evident that the effects must be significant. However, if tests were 'universal' and so intrinsically more accessible for autistic children and other pupils with SEND, this could certainly help, especially if this process also included mark schemes.

In addition, much evidence points to the poor longer-term outcomes of autistic children on a range of measures, suggesting that there is an urgent need to reconsider the question of educational priorities. There also appears to be a general failure to consult with autistic children – whose views might be at odds with those of their parents or school staff – about what matters to them. Indeed, and notwithstanding the importance placed on the views of parents and children in recent legislation (e.g. *Children and Families Act (CFA)* 2014), whether or not autistic children are engaged in the full curriculum seems to be entirely the purview of the school staff, with little or no consultation with anyone else. And so, a blanket model of desired outcomes should not be applied, and the assumption should not be made that what matters to school staff also matters to the children. Therefore, the issue is not so much what the educational priorities of autistic children should be, but how those very decisions are reached.

Key points

- Educational priorities should always be linked to questions about outcomes. Decisions about what those desired outcomes are should be reached collaboratively by school staff, parents and the child.

- The child's interests and longer-term ambitions should be an important factor in this process.

- Decisions about educational priorities and longer-term outcomes should not be based on a generalised notion of autism, but on the individual child.

- It should be recognised that excluding autistic children from part of the curriculum is a major decision, as is excluding them from assessment processes.

- School staff should familiarise themselves with the array of access arrangements for tests which are available and implement them when relevant.

Chapter 5

Learning and Cognition

Introduction

We have seen so far in this book that autistic children in schools have a lot stacked against them in terms of their well-being, progress and overall inclusion. They can be negatively impacted by the sensory onslaught that a school environment typically brings, meaning they can feel uncomfortable, distressed and unable to concentrate. They might be working on alternative targets to the rest of their class, and so trying to focus while the other children are noisily engaged in something else. And, as will be explored in more detail in Chapter 7, the autistic children may well be spending more time with the TA than the person who is qualified to teach them, the class teacher (Dockrell *et al.* 2012). They might also be missing lessons, parts of lessons, or even be temporarily or permanently excluded from the school itself. None of this augurs well for their educational progress. Indeed, it goes without saying that to make progress educationally, it does actually help to be *receiving an education.*

Sadly, these considerations are rarely factored into discussions about the poor academic achievement of autistic children in schools. Difficulties in learning and making progress are assumed, unquestioningly, to stem from autism itself, the 'within-child' factors I have described, rather than the highly problematic circumstances in which autistic children are expected to grapple with their learning.

So in this chapter, in order to try to shed some light on these issues, I explore first of all the idea of specialist teaching approaches and consider whether these are applicable to autistic children in schools. I also discuss what some consider to be an autistic thinking style or cognitive disposition – monotropism – and reflect on whether this holds the key to enabling autistic children to flourish in their learning, as well as making life easier for the adults who support them. In addition, I consider the extent to which autistic children might have learning disabilities, as well as the problems inherent to assessments of intelligence, which do not necessarily permit the true abilities of some children to be manifest.

Specialist pedagogies

Do autistic children require a different teaching approach to other children? Whitaker (2007, p.170), for example, is of the view that for autistic children, 'the means by which they learn and need to be taught may be significantly different from the majority of children'. Jones *et al.* (2008, p.14) also consider that teaching methods that rely on pupils being able 'to understand the language and social behaviour of teaching staff and other children' can be problematic for autistic children. Meanwhile, Wing (2007, p.31) considers that all autistic children 'need specialist techniques of teaching if they are to learn', and uses this to argue for the placement of many autistic children in special schools, where she believes they would be in receipt of such expertise.

■ It's important to adapt teaching methods to best accommodate the pupils' diversity and learning requirements. (Michael)

However, for Thomas and O'Hanlon (2005) (in Lewis and Norwich 2005), the need for specialist methods in the broader context of SEND is debatable, and they suggest that such approaches might, in fact, contribute to further exclude some children. Ravet (2011) also rejects the notion of 'special pedagogies', as for her, they consolidate the idea that some children need 'special' teachers in 'special' contexts, thus enabling mainstream teachers 'to absolve themselves from the responsibility of teaching them' (2011, p.672). Furthermore, Norwich and Lewis (2007) question how genuinely specialised teaching for pupils with SEND actually is, and argue that alternative pedagogical approaches can too easily lead to different learning objectives for some children.

Norwich and Lewis (2007) also describe how teaching and therapeutic interventions are a 'grey area' for pupils with SEND, meaning that the two are not clearly delineated. Jordan (2005, p.113) similarly calls for an end to 'the therapeutic model of education as a form of "treatment"', whereby the education of autistic children is considered to be a type of therapy. Therefore, the very idea of specialist teaching approaches for autistic children can, in fact, be a driver of separation and exclusion, placing some children into the category of 'other', removing them from the aims and expectations for pupils not considered to have SEND.

At the same time, however, school teachers are under a lot of pressure to be able to accommodate and understand how to teach a diversity of pupils who might have varying ways of processing information and learning. In the *Teachers' Standards* (DfE 2011), for example, a set of core principles that all teachers in England must adhere to, it is asserted that teachers should 'have a clear understanding of the needs of all pupils' including 'those with special educational needs; those of high ability; those with English as an additional language; those with disabilities' (2011, p.12). In addition, according to these rules, all teachers must 'be able to use and evaluate distinctive teaching approaches to engage and support' all pupils (DfE 2011, p.12). This is a big ask, in my view. Indeed, in my study I was sometimes struck by how many different types of equipment, materials and planning teachers were having to use for a single lesson in order to accommodate the various learners in their class.

The situation is arguably even more difficult for school SENCOs who, according to the *Code of Practice* (DfE 2015a), are responsible for ensuring that teachers in a school are able to employ different teaching styles for the range of pupils in their class. Unfortunately for them, however, although the *Code of Practice* is full of instructions about what SENCOs *must do*, there is little by way of advice about *how* they might achieve it (Allan and Youdell 2017). And so, even if you support the idea of specialist teaching approaches for autistic children, there is little information about what these approaches should actually be.

Therefore, the idea of specialist pedagogies must be approached with caution, and school staff should ensure that they have both a clear idea of what these actually are and that these approaches do not further exclude and stigmatise autistic children. Nevertheless, it can often help autistic children if learning targets are made very concrete, with tasks conveyed unambiguously, and supported by physical items when relevant, as discussed in Chapter 2. As always, though, the key message is not to generalise, and to respond to the learning needs of each child as an individual.

> I like to figure things out myself by trial and error. (Kabie)

> LEGO® and computers have a rather hands-on actually doing it approach, and that's how I learn, not reading, flicking through, but to actually do something. Sometimes I would have to have things explained to me differently than other children because I wouldn't understand what they meant. Sometimes I needed to know why we were doing it. I believe it was the language – it would be stuff they believed everyone knew and which they hadn't actually explained. (George)

> Yes. It's not by reading, but by looking and holding. More practical. I had to contextualise it. I had to corroborate it from an alternative source. I systemised things. (Jon)

Monotropism

So how do autistic children learn? Well, a key concept, promoted mainly by autistic scholars, is 'monotropism', which is described as a tendency to focus on a single issue or activity, in depth, to the exclusion of all others (Lawson 2011; Murray, Lesser and Lawson 2005). A person who is monotropic in their thinking style might have a relatively small number of areas of interest, but they are experienced in a very deep and compelling way (Milton 2012b). Indeed, although monotropism can result in a difficulty in shifting attention from the area to interest to another (Murray *et al.* 2005), it appears to be a more positive way of describing autistic cognition, setting aside pejorative terms such as 'fixated' or 'obsessive', for example (Wood 2019). This cognitive disposition can be compared with 'polytropism', which denotes a tendency to attend to a number of activities or issues (sometimes called 'multi-tasking'), but these are inevitably explored in less depth and with little sense of urgent preoccupation (Murray 2014).

Monotropism presents autistic pupils in schools, and the teachers who teach them, with a certain difficulty (Ravet 2011), especially in the earlier stages of education, where the emphasis tends to be on the need for a 'broad and balanced' curriculum (Alexander 2000). Indeed, over half of the school staff in my study said that the main reason for providing additional support for the autistic children was to keep them on task, as they were either distracted, or wished to focus on some other activity of much greater interest to them. Many school staff, and some of the parents, felt that autistic people are inherently 'obsessive' or set in their ways, showing that when a monotropic thinking style collides with an inflexible education system (Glashan *et al.* 2004), difficulties arise. And so, if an autistic child has strong interests in certain areas, and these don't fit in with the school curriculum, it will be very hard work for school staff to try to persuade them to focus on something else, as well as potentially distressing for the children if they are simply unable to shift their attention.

■ I like to talk about history, but they say, 'not now James'. I know all about James Cagney and all about history. (James, 8)

■ I don't really get to do my hobbies at school. (Rose, 8)

However, some have argued that a monotropic thinking style should not only be accommodated, but also embraced and even celebrated. Lawson (2011, p.41), for example, posited that autism should be thought of 'as a cognitive difference or style', and presented the theory of Single Attention and Associated Cognition in Autism (SAACA). Lawson (2011) argues that autistic cognition simply operates differently from non-autistic intelligence, and that current educational systems fail to accommodate this difference. In addition, this intense concentration has been associated with a deep sense of well-being, or 'flow states' (McDonnell and Milton 2014; Wood and Milton 2018). So, given that specialising is currently only considered desirable at the later stages of education, let us now consider how we can harness the monotropic thinking style of autistic children in our school system in order to facilitate their inclusion.

The inclusionary power of interests
Perhaps unsurprisingly, given the apparent difficulties of getting autistic children to focus and concentrate on teacher-led activities, I found that they can be subject to rather heavy-duty and over-directive prompting, both physically and verbally, in order to keep them on task (Wood 2019). This issue, which will be covered in more detail in Chapter 7, is surely a highly unsatisfactory state of affairs for all concerned.

However, one of the most striking findings from my study was the extent to which enabling autistic children to incorporate their interests (sometimes called 'special interests' or 'restricted interests') into their learning not only addresses the core issue of concentration and motivation, but also means that school staff don't need to keep prompting them to stay on task. Indeed, being able to focus deeply on their areas of interest appeared to provide a range of positive functions for the autistic children, including helping them to cope with the stress of school, improved communication, better access to the curriculum and tests, greater independence, more socialisation and overall enjoyment of school. Therefore, I found that actively embracing the monotropic thinking style of autistic children often helps, rather than hinders, school staff and the autistic pupils.

> I'm rather interested in my LEGO® and my computer. Something I definitely do every day. I feel somewhat detached from the world around me when I am doing these things, which makes a nice break. It's quite structural and logical. (George)

> The one thing that was inclusive was that certain teachers – I did better in their classes. They were more progressive, they took note of my interests, and so I learned very quickly. (Jon)

> There needs to be much more flexibility. Also a greater understanding that autistic kids may not be motivated about the same things or in the same way as non-autistic kids. (Kabie)

There is, in fact, a growing body of research evidence to support the idea that, despite a few drawbacks, enabling autistic children to have access to and develop their areas of interest is highly beneficial for their education and broader inclusion in school (Gunn and Delafield-Butt 2016). Wittemeyer *et al.* (2011b), for example, assert that encouraging the interests of autistic children can facilitate the forming of good relationships and lead to an increase in curriculum access and learning, a point also made by Hesmondhalgh and Breakey (2001). Gunn and Delafield-Butt (2016), in a review of the literature, state that most studies show a strong, positive correlation between incorporating the interests of autistic children into the classroom and improved learning and social skills, while Jones *et al.* (2008) argue that the strong interests of autistic children can facilitate participation in after-school clubs. Similarly, Winter-Messiers (2007) found strong positive links between the interests of the autistic children and young people and their social and communication abilities, as well as their emotional well-being and fine motor skills. Therefore, it's important to perceive monotropism and the tendency to have intense interests as a strength, rather than a deficit (Boyd, Woodward and Bodfish 2011). This conceptualisation also allows a more positive framing of repetitive behaviour (McDonnell and Milton 2014), which, as we saw in Chapter 1, is typically viewed as a problem associated with autism (Baron-Cohen and Wheelwright 1999).

> Art is my passion. I love to draw and spend a lot of time doing it in and out of school and animation is really fun. Sci-fi and action are my favourite genres, so I watch a lot of those movies/shows and sometimes wildlife/nature documentaries because I love animals. I am very interested in the conservation of Big Cats in the wild and protecting them from being hunted and I find them quite fascinating in general (tigers are my favourites). (Grace, 14)

> Utterly important. I call them special interests. I wouldn't exist as a person if those interests weren't me. My interest in planets and space saved my life – something out of school, e.g. looking at the skies, enabled me to learn. I used those specialist interests, to save me from dwelling on it. Because at school I was being told I was useless. This prevented me from becoming naughty, difficult or unwell. (Jon)

> I do like chickens, so I decided to make an app about it. You have to try and smack chickens with a really good hammer. But you can upgrade the chickens when you get coins, and then you can keep up upgrading to a better chicken the more coins you get, so you end up with a city, and then an empire. There are 1 million levels. It's still a work in progress. (Rose, 8)

I will illustrate this point in relation to one particular boy in my own study, who was aged 10 at the time. He generally found the school curriculum very difficult, and his own learning activities were significantly differentiated to a level much lower than that of his chronological year group. In fact, they were set at pre-school level, and his TA, a dedicated and enthusiastic person, tried very hard, using a range of techniques, to get him to progress in his studies.

But he seemed really quite lost during these activities, and any sort of advancement appeared to elude him. He was, however, very keen on football, and to see him play with his classmates was to tell a very different story. Here, he required no support whatsoever, and, in fact, took a leading role in the game, calling to his team mates about where they should place themselves, anticipating the moves of others, reacting quickly to sudden changes of ball direction and the actions of other players. One can only imagine the difference assessments of his ability levels would show in relation to Maths, for example, compared with football. Of course, this boy may well have had some sort of a learning disability, but when he was engaged in his great interest – football – he was far from disabled, but rather skilled, agile and astute.

- My major interest at primary age was dogs: breed standards including sizes and temperament – everything there was to know. At the time if anything at all at school could be twisted to somehow involve dogs I was delighted and much more enthusiastic about the work. Using interests to make learning more attractive is definitely useful. (Kabie)

- I've always been interested in music (having come from a musical family) and I have an in-depth knowledge of Judo, having practised the sport for 16 years. (Michael)

Fortunately, some school staff in my study understood the benefits of harnessing the interests of the autistic children. One teacher, for example, used a child's strong interest in Disney films to set him different curriculum activities and tests. Indeed, because she also shared his interest, she felt that this mutual pursuit created a special bond between them. Recognising and valuing their shared interests therefore resulted in the opposite of 'othering', whereby rather than seeing the autistic boy as somehow different to her, the teacher perceived both of them as being of a similar kind (Wood 2019).

- What we did to help me bond with my future teacher was finding a common interest, in my case, Star Wars. Clone Wars was something we were both interested in and what helped convince me that he was actually interested in Star Wars were some bits of Star Wars LEGO® he had in his classroom. Seeing those same LEGO® pieces still in the classroom on the first day also helped me not be so nervous because I knew I had something in common with the teacher and something we could talk about together. (Grace, 14)

Nevertheless, school staff identified some drawbacks to this disposition. Some teachers commented that they found it difficult to persuade the autistic children to focus on certain curriculum subjects, or were concerned that in tests, they would write about their preoccupations rather than answering the questions. Indeed, it is worth considering if this phenomenon is another factor in the poor test results obtained by autistic children in national assessments, as discussed in the last chapter. Moreover, the broader literature suggests that very intense interests can be associated negatively with well-being (Grove *et al.* 2018), as there is a fine line between 'flow' and 'negatively experienced compulsions' (McDonnell and Milton 2014, p.45).

Even so, despite the fact that strong interests can sometimes create barriers to learning and access to tests for autistic children, I found that the positive impacts from enabling them to focus on their interests were much more numerous. Importantly, school staff also benefited, as they demonstrated better skills, prompted the children less and were generally less intrusive in their support in these circumstances too. In addition, a number of my autistic research participants associated their interests with a high level of skill and expertise, as well as laying a path for their future career. This shows that there can be important longer-term benefits of enabling autistic children to access their interests in school (Grove *et al.* 2018; Jones *et al.* 2008), as well as those evident in the shorter term too.

My interest in dinosaurs was about my interest in the world, and where I fitted in. That's why it saved my life when I was at school. It gave me an anchor point that was real and solid, not people's impression. (Jon)

And so, while it must be recognised that in the current education system, school staff operate within certain constraints, if they can find ways to imaginatively tap into the interests of autistic children, this would certainly make life easier for everyone. Indeed, it goes without saying that all children will work better and more independently if they are engaged in an activity that interests and motivates them (Hidi and Renniger 2006), and so working out how to support the interests of autistic children could benefit other children too. This suggests that, notwithstanding the issues concerning a modified curriculum discussed in the previous chapter, teachers should be able to adopt a flexible approach to the teaching and learning of the pupils in their class.

- Interests – it's definitely something, from what I've experienced of myself and others, it will be something we can be incredibly knowledgeable about. (George)

- I'm not 100 per cent sure just yet what I want to do when I am grown up, but I would like to go either down the path of artist/ animator or animal conservationist as they are the things I am most passionate about. (Grace, 14)

- So picking up that first fossil when I was six meant I trained to be a palaeontologist. I did my degree, I was very specialised, I was going to do a PhD on fossil sharks, but there were problems, and I pulled out. I became an illustrator (geological book illustrating), so I sort of combined the two. That led on to doing archaeological illustration. Now I'm an artist, but I use my special interests in time, archaeology and geology in art. (Jon)

- Special interests are of paramount importance – not only to get some time out but they can be used as an important learning tool. They can also forge a clear career path and ignoring special interests can lead to extreme boredom or disinterest. (Michael)

Autism and assessments of ability

Just how many autistic children and adults also have an intellectual or learning disability is unclear, especially as the prevalence figures on this vary greatly. Buescher et al. (2014), for example, assume a rate of 40 per cent in the UK and the USA, while Vivanti et al. (2013)

put the figure at two-thirds of all autistic people. In a Danish study, Knüppel, Telléus and Lauritsen (2018) found a rate of 16.7 per cent of intellectual disability amongst their participants who were diagnosed with autism before the age of 14, although this was nearly 29 per cent for those diagnosed before the age of 7. These figures compare with those found by the National Academy of Sciences (2015) in the USA, where prevalence studies of intellectual disabilities revealed rates of between 8.7 to 36.8 per 1,000 (i.e. between 0.9 and 3.7%) of all children. So it does seem apparent that a significant proportion of autistic children – although by no means all – might have an additional learning disability.

In 2001, the Department of Health in the UK defined learning disability as 'a significantly reduced ability to understand new or complex information, to learn new skills (impaired intelligence)' (DH 2001, p.14), combined with impaired social functioning, with these issues having been evident since childhood. So it's not hard to see why the lines between autism and learning disabilities might become blurred in certain diagnostic contexts, especially as some studies focus on the extent to which children with a learning disability might also meet the criteria for autism (Deb and Prasad 1994). Nevertheless, the latest version of the ICD (the ICD-11; WHO 2018) states that 'individuals along the spectrum exhibit a full range of intellectual functioning', showing that the assumption must not be made that autistic children are also intellectually disabled.[1]

However, many studies proceed unquestioningly on the basis that autism is a sub-category of a range of developmental disabilities (Boyle et al. 2011) and presuppose that, by dint of having a diagnosis of autism, children must also have learning disabilities. Indeed, the assumption that autistic people are cognitively impaired 'pervades the popular and scientific literature' (Dawson et al. 2007, p.657), and is deeply entrenched within professional medical and educational communities. Even high abilities are considered to be indicative of yet further dysfunction (Dawson et al. 2007), or somehow exotic or strange (Arnold 2013). And so autistic people can't really win: they are either considered intellectually sub-standard or weirdly gifted.

---

1   https://icd.who.int/browse11/l-m/en#/http://id.who.int/icd/entity/437815624

Not only this, but assessments of intelligence are another minefield through which autistic children rarely tiptoe unscathed. Dawson *et al.* (2007), for example, demonstrated how the widely used assessment tool – the Wechsler Intelligence Scales – results in an underestimation of the intelligence of autistic people, particularly those with minimal verbal ability. Indeed, if autistic people with few verbal skills are unquestioningly assumed to be 'low functioning' (Courchesne *et al.* 2018; Dawson *et al.* 2007), tests that 'measure factual knowledge, expressive language abilities, and short-term memory' can unfairly and negatively skew the results of some children (Siegel 1989, p.469).

Unsurprisingly, these problems also impact on certain school subjects. Siegel (1989), for example, considers that IQ test scores cannot reliably identify learning disabilities, and that a low score doesn't necessarily indicate impaired reading skills either. Moreover, according to Johnston (1985), the assumption that reading difficulties derive from cognitive impairment, rather than 'the individual's goals, motives, and situations' (1985, p.154), leads to inappropriate analysis of that failure. Campbell (2015) also found that the very labelling of a pupil with 'SEND' influences teacher assessments. She reports that, as a result of 'teacher-level bias' (2015, p.518), pupils with a diagnosis of SEND are more likely to be judged as 'below average' in Maths compared with children without such a diagnosis.

Furthermore, according to Thomas (2012), assessments of learning disability are always relative, and emerge from comparisons between pupils, meaning that some will always be deemed to be sub-standard. Indeed, Croll (2002) found that such assessments are at least in part socially determined, as they are measured in accordance with the social and academic norms within the educational setting where the child is placed. As a result, a child in one school might be considered to have a learning disability but not in another.

Not only this, but Armstrong, Galloway and Tomlinson (1993) found that children sometimes consider the assessment process itself to be some sort of punishment. This can impact negatively on how they perform, a phenomenon that is then misinterpreted by those carrying out the assessment. Armstrong *et al.* (1993) argue further that associated professionals, conflicted by different loyalties – to their employer, the school, the child's parents – 'often felt constrained to define the problem in terms of difficulties the child presented to others' (1993, p.128), rather than engaging with the child's perspective. Therefore, they argue, important questions are raised about the ways in which professionals carrying out assessments both construct and represent 'childhood deviance' (1993, p.130).

These issues all show the extent to which determining the abilities and cognitive impairments of autistic children is fraught with difficulties and complications. While it is clear that some autistic children have some sort of a learning disability, the assumption should not be made that this applies to all. It is therefore essential to adopt a holistic and flexible approach to assessments of intelligence (Courchesne *et al.* 2018), incorporating any environmental factors, assumptions and bias, and whether or not the test itself is suitable for the child. Dawson *et al.* (2007), for example, found that the Raven's Progressive Matrices, an intelligence test that does not rely on verbal input, can enable the abilities of autistic children and adults to be more fairly measured.

Conclusion

While the evidence for specialist teaching approaches for autistic children is not clear, there are some general considerations to bear in mind in order to make the classroom a more welcoming space for them. First of all, the general school environment must be comfortable for autistic children, as they will simply not feel at ease or able to concentrate if their energies are taken up with trying to cope with the sensory onslaught that excessive noise creates, for example. Communication should be unambiguous, and teachers should be aware that their instructions will not necessarily be interpreted in the same way by all children. Furthermore, if it is not clear how many autistic children have an additional learning disability, the assumption that they are all cognitively impaired should not be made.

In addition, it is useful for school staff to support and encourage the typical thinking style of autistic children and to try to incorporate their interests into their learning, tests and social activities, even if limitations to the curriculum mean this is difficult. Indeed, teachers and support staff could find considerable benefits from encouraging the interests of autistic children, if they employ creative and imaginative approaches in the classroom. For example, a child who is intensely interested in insects could carry out an extended topic on this subject, with the teacher building in Maths, English, Art, Science and ICT at the same time. With such an approach, school staff could be facilitating considerably the longer-term outcomes and career ambitions of the autistic children, as well as creating the circumstances within which they can develop their own skills as teachers. In these ways, other children stand to benefit too. However, school staff should be aware that it can be very difficult for autistic children to switch their attention to something else, especially without warning, and that interests experienced on a very intense level can be distressing.

In the next chapter, I consider core school subjects in more detail, and discuss the extent to which they are accessible or not for autistic children. I also provide suggestions as to how to improve access, engagement and attainment in those subjects.

Key points

- School staff should ensure that the classroom environment is conducive to the learning and well-being of the autistic children.

- Incorporating the interests of the autistic children in all aspects of their time in school can be highly beneficial for both children and staff. However, there can be disadvantages to a monotropic thinking style.

- The assumption that autistic children have learning disabilities should not be made.

- Assessments should be holistic, incorporating the perspectives of the child if possible. Using appropriate assessment instruments is key.

- Assessments should be child-centred, rather than serving the requirements of the adults.

Chapter 6

The Curriculum

Introduction

In Chapter 2, we discussed the ways in which sensory phenomena can impact on autistic children in school, making it difficult for them to concentrate, and even creating distress. Then, in Chapter 3, we looked at the complexities of inclusion, and the fact that autistic children might be on a patchy, part-time educational schedule, with limited access to extra-curricular activities. Or they might even be excluded from school altogether.

And in Chapter 4, we considered the educational priorities of autistic children, and how therapeutic input, for example, can be confused with learning targets, meaning they miss out on opportunities to gain qualifications. Meanwhile, in the last chapter, we discussed how the ways in which autistic children think, learn and respond to their environment (Lawson 2011) might be at odds with typical expectations in the classroom, while assessments of ability run the risk of underestimating their strengths (Dawson *et al.* 2007). And even though enabling autistic children to access their interests in school has been shown to bring a range of benefits (Wood 2019), the combination of all of these other factors means that many autistic children struggle in school, sometimes dropping out of the system altogether.

 Because we're wired differently, because we absorb information differently, we end up dropping out. (Jon)

Therefore, let us now turn to specific school subjects, and consider the hurdles and difficulties autistic children face, while suggesting some solutions to these problems. I focus on Phonics, Reading, Writing, Maths and PE because these are the subjects on which I was mainly able to collect data in the schools for my study. These are all areas that merit whole chapters and even books in their own right, and so I only concentrate on the aspects that most stood out in my study. In addition, because my data collection was based mainly in primary schools, some examples here are specific to that age group, although there are certainly lessons for later educational stages too.

Phonics

It's difficult to know where to start with Phonics. Embraced for many years now within the UK education system as the go-to method for teaching children how to read (DfE 2014), it's a topic that is nevertheless the source of much debate. While there is certainly evidence to support the efficacy of Phonics as a method (Brady 2011), this approach has become something of a religion, with its numerous acolytes unable to contemplate any other way of teaching children how to read. Sadly, the few who dare to question the wholesale endorsement of this method are dismissed as 'Phonics deniers', a term worryingly evocative of 'climate change deniers', or even 'Holocaust deniers'. Such an extreme positioning, and dismissing the detractors of this approach as suffering from 'Phonics phobia', is unhelpful to all children, and for those who do not learn language this way, pretty disastrous.

So, what is Phonics? In simple terms, it involves matching the sounds of spoken English with individual letters or groups of letters (National Literacy Trust 2017). There are different types of Phonics, but they all centre on this core, aural approach, which in itself immediately raises questions about its accessibility for visual learners, for example. Certainly, the statistics from the DfE are very telling from the point of view of autistic children, who do not appear to find Phonics especially helpful or accessible. Between 2012 and 2016, 81 per cent of all pupils in primary schools were assessed as meeting the required standard of Phonics decoding by the end of Year 1, 18 per cent did not meet the standard, and 2 per cent of all primary schoolchildren were disapplied from the test (DfE 2016a). However, only 36 per cent of autistic pupils met the standard, 34 per cent did not, and a whopping 30 per cent were disapplied from the test itself (DfE 2016a).

Furthermore, between 2013 and 2016, the situation by the end of Year 2 – when pupils can be tested again or for the first time – was that 91 per cent of all primary school pupils met the standard in Phonics decoding, 7 per cent did not, and 1 per cent had no result recorded (DfE 2016a). However, while the statistics for autistic pupils also showed an improvement – 51 per cent met the standard, while 24 per cent did not – a staggering 24 per cent had no result recorded (DfE 2016a). This means that by the end of Year 1, the majority of autistic children – 64 per cent – were not coping with Phonics, while by the end of Year 2, nearly half – 48 per cent – continued to experience this difficulty.

Of course, we must bear in mind that these are comparisons between groups of greatly different sizes: there are over 600,000 primary school pupils in total compared with the significantly lower figure of nearly 7,000 autistic pupils in those schools. And so, these sorts of statistics must be approached with caution, especially those from the DfE, which regularly changes how it presents data (DfE 2015b). However, when combined with smaller-scale qualitative data, from studies such as mine, which showed that most of the 10 autistic children were unable to access Phonics, and that such an approach even creates problems with spelling, this does indicate a major issue for autistic pupils in schools.

So why do autistic children find Phonics difficult? Well, for starters, if they have language processing difficulties, or tend to learn visually or experientially rather than aurally, Phonics as a method for learning how to read is unlikely to work for them.

▦ I think I'm quite a visual learner. I'm not great at processing verbal information and then knowing what to do – printed step-by-step instructions work better for me. If I want to learn how to do something now, watching a YouTube video or looking it up online works way better than asking someone to explain to me. (Kabie)

▦ Autistic people tend to be visual or experiential learners. This very much depends on the individual. (Michael)

In addition, one deputy head teacher suggested that because Phonics is a system that can result in the production of non-words, the illogicality of this can confuse autistic children, especially if they are 'literal' thinkers (Humphrey and Symes 2011). Indeed, research shows that autistic children struggle with decoding non-words (Nation *et al.* 2006), and find it difficult to consolidate both phonological and semantic information (Norbury, Griffiths and Nation 2010).

Another problem that seemed evident in my study was that Phonics was typically taught with all children seated hugger-mugger 'on the carpet': autistic children can find this difficult, because sensory issues make close proximity to large groups of people uncomfortable (Bogdashina 2016). Not only this, but I also noticed that teachers and TAs switched between enunciating phonemes or reciting the alphabet in a more traditional manner, suggesting a certain degree of confusion on their part about Phonics. In fact, it's worth bearing in mind that as Phonics was only introduced in the UK about 20 or so years ago, there are whole generations of school staff – including those who were educated in other countries – who managed to learn how to read without Phonics, and indeed, who might not even understand it fully. And so, it might be the case that some autistic children – who tend to spend more time than their peers on their own with support staff (Millar *et al.* 2002) – struggle with Phonics because those helping them don't understand it either.

I don't doubt that Phonics can be successful for some, even a lot of, children. However, for many autistic children, Phonics appears to be little more than a source of frustration and confusion, which potentially delays their progress and interrupts their reading pleasure. Indeed, most of the children in my study were able readers, but had apparently learned this skill through 'whole word recognition', and despite, rather than because of, Phonics.

Reading

All of the autistic children in my study, to a greater or lesser extent, derived a great deal of pleasure from books, especially – although not uniquely – if they had a high visual content, and accorded with their areas of interest. I took books with me on all of my visits to the schools, and they were a useful 'ice-breaker' when I was getting to know the children. Indeed, some of these children, described as disengaged or with patchy concentration, would settle down contentedly with a book, requiring little or no additional support from an adult. So, if reading for pleasure – associated with a range of educational, affective and socio-economic advantages (DfE 2012) – is the ultimate aim of school reading programmes, the children in my study seemed well on their way to achieving this goal.

> Reading, I thought that this was amazing: pick up a book, absorb all of that information that someone else had written. It meant I could learn anything that I wanted to and didn't need anyone else to help. I was reading factual books, I particularly liked dictionaries and encyclopaedias, as well as dog books – of course! (Kabie)

However, reading ability is another complex area when considered in the context of autistic cognition, and has been the subject of a great deal of research, much of it highly technical and beyond the scope of my own study. For example, difficulties in oral language and social skills are considered to impact negatively on reading aptitude (Dockrell *et al.* 2012; Ricketts *et al.* 2013), and autistic children are thought to lack the ability to make inferences (Norbury and Nation 2011) and to have limited ability in reading comprehension (Nation *et al.* 2006).

Indeed, autistic children who possess a broad vocabulary are deemed to understand language on a superficial, almost mechanistic, level only. Such children, it is considered, might recognise the words but they don't really *understand* them in a deep and nuanced way (Dockrell *et al.* 2012; Jones *et al.* 2008). Nation *et al.* (2006), for example, set out the difference between word recognition and reading comprehension, arguing that even if autistic children have an exceptionally high level of word identification – that is, they are hyperlexic – they do not necessarily possess the concomitant understanding of the meanings of this extensive vocabulary:

> Such apparently well-developed reading skills are usually only superficial. Reading accuracy is well-developed and precocious but reading comprehension is severely impaired. (Nation *et al.* 2006, p.912)

The authors also argue that autistic children show difficulties in phonological decoding, a skill they consider essential to 'normal reading development' (Nation *et al.* 2006, p.912). This, at the very least, might indicate why autistic children struggle with Phonics, and suggests that they should be supported in learning how to read by alternative methods.

> I am dyslexic but was not diagnosed until the age of 39. I dreaded spelling tests, grammar (even though I was good at systemising – I learned Latin myself because I had to learn what the dinosaurs' names meant) and comprehension. I knew I wasn't stupid, but I was incapable of demonstrating that to the teacher. I actually taught myself to read with Commando war comics. I taught myself under the covers with a torch. (Jon)

I also found in my own study that in reading exercises and tests, autistic children can fall foul of the requirement to make inferences, whereby they are expected to anticipate what might happen next, or make connected assumptions, based on written or sometimes visual materials. Educators set a great deal of store by this, as it is supposed to represent some sort of higher-level thinking, indicating that children can expand from the text and develop ideas and sequences of thought intellectually (Kispal 2008). Consequently, children who are considered unable to do this are also thought to lack cognitive skill and, as we have seen, to be superficial readers only (Norbury and Nation 2011). Combined with this is the view that autistic children might be literal thinkers, whereby idioms, metaphorical language and factually conflicting information create confusion and misunderstandings. Indeed, this certainly seems to apply to at least some autistic people, as our contributor Michael has written about in his own books (Barton 2012). The result for autistic children in primary schools, therefore, can be that they make different assumptions based on the materials presented, or are confused by seemingly contradictory written and visual clues. But does this mean that a literal way of interpreting these materials is somehow of a lesser order?

"How do you know it is raining?"

Let's take Sonny's illustration above as an example. The boy is looking at a picture of a dinosaur holding an umbrella and the question is 'How do you know it is raining?' This hypothetical scenario could be quite confusing to certain sorts of logical and literal thinkers. After all, dinosaurs are extinct, and when they roamed the earth, they didn't use umbrellas. And so, even if you think the answer to the comprehension question is obvious, I hope you get my point that an autistic child might be stumped by this.

Of course, some children genuinely do find making inferences, or predicting what might happen next, quite difficult. But for some of the children in my study, it was more a case of using different information to make alternative, unanticipated predictions, although these unanticipated predictions were not necessarily considered valid by school staff.

It's also worth considering whether assessments of reading ability are based on expectations of what non-autistic children might do. What might, in fact, be taking place, at least some of the time, is that autistic children are unable to demonstrate their understanding in a way deemed acceptable, and that their response to written material is at variance with established norms. Moreover, according to Colenbrander, Nickels and Kohnen (2017), different assessment instruments, which apparently assess the same reading skills, can yield different results. The Neale Analysis of Reading Ability (NARA), for example, relies more on decoding skills than the York Assessment of Reading for Comprehension (YARC), and so, they argue, 'a single comprehension assessment can never capture the complexity associated with reading comprehension ability' (Colenbrander et al. 2017, p.416).

Certainly, the national statistics for Reading at primary school level indicate that this is an area that needs to be addressed in order to ensure parity of access for autistic children. In 2016, for example, only 36 per cent of autistic pupils in England achieved the expected standard in Reading, compared with 66 per cent of all pupils (DfE 2017a). At GCSE level, the results are similar, with only 31 per cent of autistic pupils achieving A*–C grades in English and Maths, compared with 63 per cent of all pupils (DfE 2017b).

■ English (was difficult) – things such as words having different spellings and the spelling of words not making sense, and words having different meanings. (George)

■ My reading was very poor, but I was bright. I was taken out of class for 'retarded reading lessons'. I got teased mercilessly by other children because of my problems in reading. But if I got something right, I was a swot. (Jon)

■ English was beyond me and made me annoyed and bored. I would rather have done anything else! (Michael)

Some teachers commented that the autistic children would only engage with books they had chosen themselves, which created problems in curriculum access. Difficulties also emerged when the adult supporting the child was over-directive with the reading activity, especially if also attempting to dictate what should be of interest to the child and how the narrative should be interpreted. Sometimes, well-meaning TAs were observed to be interrupting and distracting autistic children when they were absorbed in books, as well as coercing the children to focus on aspects of the book they had less interest in. Imagine if you were engrossed in reading your favourite novel, and someone started firing questions at you, or asked you to turn back a few pages, to answer some questions on synonyms or punctuation that bore little relation to what you were enjoying about the book. I suspect you wouldn't like it too much.

Almost all the time I don't like Literacy. It's boring and lame. All about commas and writing more neatly. Urgh. And sentences and what you end sentences with, punctuation – it's really boring. I hate it. (Rose, 8)

Of course, teachers must teach, and there is a time for this, but it should also be recognised that if a child is contentedly engrossed in reading a book, then ideally the message should be 'Do not disturb'. Moreover, we mustn't create a situation where having choice in reading materials is a luxury we only permit in adulthood.

Maths

As we have seen already, the results for autistic pupils in national tests are significantly poorer than for all pupils in Reading and English, and the picture is similar for Maths. For example, at Key Stage 2 in 2016, only 36 per cent of autistic pupils reached the expected standard in Maths, but 70 per cent of all pupils in primary schools reached this level (DfE 2017a). So here, too, it appears that autistic children are struggling to access this subject in school. Even so, and as we saw in the last chapter, Campbell (2015) found that as a result of teacher bias, pupils with the label of 'SEND' are more likely to be assessed as below average in Maths, suggesting that for some children at least, their skills are being underestimated at classroom level.

In my own study, my findings in relation to Maths were quite mixed. Some of the autistic adults had excelled in the subject, and one of them was considered to be gifted. Amongst the autistic children, some really enjoyed Maths, while one boy demonstrated exceptional aptitude, saying, for example, that one of his favourite activities was doing fractions. In fact, Maths permeated all of his leisure activities, and the formulation of numbers influenced his attitudes towards school subjects, his social activities and different aspects of the school day. He also created number puzzles to calm himself in times of stress, a process that fortunately was understood and supported by his class teacher.

> Maths was logical, different from English, where there are confusing answers. With Maths, everything is specific, there is a right answer. It was easier. It was the one subject where I was actually in the same class as other people because the teacher actually got me. (George)

> I was quite good at maths and reading and so finished the reading scheme very quickly, I also finished primary maths early. Although I went to special maths lessons at the school once or twice a week the rest of the time when the class was doing regular Maths or English I was making the teachers' tea, organising cupboards, repainting blackboards: lots of jobs around the school. I would have preferred to have been given different maths and English things to do on my own to keep learning rather than these 'odd jobs'. (Kabie)

> Maths (was my favourite subject) because it was easy and the content taught was far below my ability. I found it interesting to learn about. Even though the content was easy it only frustrated me as I went into senior school, as my learning was quicker than the rate at which I was taught. (Michael)

However, some of the autistic adults had really struggled in Maths, with one of the adults describing herself as 'number blind'. Some of the autistic children also found Maths difficult. In addition, issues aired by school staff were that the autistic children liked to problem-solve in their own way, not in the manner dictated by the teacher. Similarly, Williams (1992/1999, p.55) stated the following in her autobiographical account: 'I learned to dislike maths as I had always done the working-out in my head but was now being told to "show the working out".'

Other problems cited were that some autistic children didn't like to estimate (preferring instead to ascertain the exact amount or sum), or would become distressed if they didn't get the answer right. Furthermore, correcting their own work, such as by crossing out mistakes, was also a difficulty for a couple of the children in my study.

▪ Hate numbers! So boring. Don't like it, it's too hard. Makes my head hurt. (James, 8)

▪ Really hard, unable to understand. (Zack, 10)

Maths was also one of the subjects where I observed a certain amount of repetition, with autistic children expected to carry out the same task, using the same materials, again and again. Crucially, I found that physical items such as number lines, weighing scales, clocks and blocks for fractions are usually withdrawn once children reach a certain level or stage in Maths, as they are expected to be able to make calculations mentally or using pen and paper. However, due to issues with proprioception (Caldwell 2008), and perhaps even a different attitude towards objects (White and Remington 2018; see also Jon's comments in Chapter 2), autistic children may well need to continue to use physical items as they progress through a Maths curriculum. Indeed, if schools want to accept and encourage a diversity of learners, it seems to me that to associate a high level of mathematical skill with the ability to make calculations without physical props is both misconceived and unhelpful.

Therefore, while it is the case that some autistic people demonstrate very high ability in Maths (Baron-Cohen *et al.* 2007), many autistic children do appear to be struggling with the subject in its current format.

Writing

All of the children in my cohort struggled with writing, either in terms of the content of the topics they were asked to write about, or the physical skills required. Even the sole child who enjoyed writing activities – the only girl in the pupil cohort – found written tasks time-consuming and effortful. It is perhaps unsurprising therefore, that at Key Stage 2, autistic pupils lag even further behind in the statistical averages, with only 35 per cent reaching the expected standard in 2016, compared with 74 per cent for all pupils (DfE 2017a).

One issue was the nature of what the children were expected to write about. For some, a strong preoccupation with a particular interest meant it was difficult for teachers to get them to write on other topics. Similarly, Williams (1992/1999, p.55) stated that in English, she would write, 'though never on the prescribed topic'. In addition, and although this was not the case for all, open questions of the 'Describe your perfect weekend' variety were found to be especially problematic, as were those aimed at encouraging some sort of creative expression.

Story writing: imagining and making up a story with no direction (was difficult). I found a blank piece of paper and the instruction 'use your imagination' ridiculous. At that age I couldn't see the point. (Kabie)

It is perhaps worth remembering that while it is important to encourage creativity in school, not all children have an inner poet waiting to burst forth. Some find beauty in details and facts, not fiction, and so the sort of writing some autistic children produce deserves to be credited with its own aesthetic, rather than measured against a narrow conceptualisation of what constitutes imaginative work.

However, it was the physical, motor skill of writing that the autistic children in my study found the most difficult (Kushki, Chau and Anagnostou 2011). Yet only two of the children, including a boy who had an additional physical disability, received support from an occupational therapist, and the extent to which this input was targeted at their difficulties with handwriting was not clear in any case. On other occasions, autistic children educated separately from their cohort were expected to write in cramped spaces, or on tables that were either too high or too low (unlike the tables and desks in their classroom), or even on the floor, creating yet more disadvantage in an area where they were already struggling. Support staff also alternated between placing pens in the child's right and left hand, without having identified which one the child preferred to use.

Moreover, if differentiated Maths exercises were sometimes repetitive and uninspiring, this problem also applied to a small number of writing exercises I observed. Tasks of zero educational value, made up on the spot, consisting predominantly of monotonous, rote copying, were evident, creating significant demoralisation on the part of the child, and even distress.

▨ I know I would get quite bored if we were doing something that was incredibly repetitive; whereas for some children that would be perfect, for me that would be boring, because I would get distracted and uninterested and wouldn't actually learn. (George)

By contrast, however, the two youngest children in my study, both aged four, benefited greatly from a sensory approach to early writing skills. Provided with brightly coloured, thick felt-tipped pens they could pick and choose, white boards they could wipe clean at will, peg boards and brushes, as well as items to colour in which corresponded with their interests, they remained absorbed and engaged with these activities for long periods. These circumstances also resulted in minimal input from the TAs, who clearly gained vicarious pleasure from the children's enjoyment of these activities.

Unfortunately, there was no equivalent for the older children who, rather like the approach to Maths and the use of physical props, were considered to no longer need this sort of tactile and motivating input. In my view, therefore, there is an urgent need to develop handwriting activities for older autistic children, incorporating some of the sensory appeal and fine and gross motor support that clearly helped the younger children.

In addition, even though many of the autistic children had a strong interest in computers and other forms of technology, there was very little consideration of the vast myriad of alternatives to handwriting, such as typing, predictive text, using a stylus and other available technological advances (McNaughton and Light 2013). Indeed, there were indications in my study that due to being placed with a TA much of the time, the autistic children had less, not more, access to computers than their peers. This is despite evidence of the ways in which technology can help further the educational inclusion of autistic children (Murray and Lawson 2007). Furthermore, most school tests and exams still rely on being able to write competently, and at speed, while primary school assessments are not yet available online.

Being unable to write well can therefore create significant barriers for children who do not possess this skill. Yet the UNCRC (UNICEF 1989) makes it clear that children must be able to express themselves freely, and that information should be imparted 'regardless of frontiers, either orally, in writing or in print, in the form of art, or through any other media of the child's choice' (Article 13).

⬛ ICT is fun because we are learning to animate and use Photoshop which is something I have always wanted to do. (Grace, 14)

PE

It had not been my original intention to collect data on PE, but a few issues emerged in relation to this school activity that merit attention. For example, some parents and school staff thought that PE could be dropped for the autistic children to make way for extra help in other subjects, or for communication interventions. Indeed, some of the autistic children had quite patchy access to this activity, mainly due to sensory issues such as sensitivity to noise or not wanting to get changed into a PE kit. Some of the autistic adults had experienced similar difficulties, and cited close proximity to other children or needing to hold hands for some games as being particularly unpleasant. In addition, teachers said that simply organising their kit, getting changed out of uniform and back again, was unsettling and difficult for the autistic children.

The social aspects of PE created further difficulties. For example, a couple of the autistic adults said that they had always been last to be chosen for teams, and I also observed one of the autistic children being ostracised by his classmates when they were instructed to choose a partner for games. Another child was heavily prompted by the TA during PE, which created a barrier between him and his peers, and the parent and teacher of another boy said that he couldn't cope with losing in games.

> Absolutely hated PE, I was very uncoordinated. I perhaps enjoyed it in the early years, but when my confidence took a hit in the 4th year, I didn't want it on show and PE was one of the areas when that would happen. I couldn't do the assault course in the right order. There weren't specific instructions, so I couldn't work out what to do. (Jon)

> For PE we had to get changed in the classroom, the gym kit was horrible sensory wise. I was bad at it: very uncoordinated. The worst thing was 'dance' as they called it which was all about imagining we were something and moving about amongst the other kids gracefully: this is so not me! In lower Primary I was always super-slow to get changed which often gained a slap on the legs (didn't make me

faster as it was a 'can't' rather than intentional slowness). Although I did after-school activities – swimming, badminton, squash – those that I did in school I hated and tried to get out of PE whenever possible. Shared changing rooms, communal showers, having to take part in things that just reminded me how bad I was at things, being shouted at, ridiculed. I remember one report that described me in PE as 'apathetic'. (Kabie)

▨ I'm impartial to PE but dislike team sports as I dislike my abilities being different to that of team mates. In other words, if I'm doing well but everybody else isn't, or vice versa, this is frustrating. With individual sports it's all about my ability and how I perform. (Michael)

However, two of the children in my study said that PE was amongst their favourite subjects in school, and even those who rarely had access to PE because of sensory issues nevertheless enjoyed physical exercise. Some of the autistic adults also valued PE and had enjoyed it at school. My contributor Zack (aged 10) said that his favourite 'subject' in school is 'being outside', and George also enjoyed PE:

▨ From what I can remember, I enjoyed PE. Instead of being sat in a classroom, or in my case, a cupboard, you were actually up and about doing stuff. It was a different change of scenery. (George)

Therefore, the picture around PE emerges as being quite complex, with a combination of sensory, organisational and social factors potentially creating significant barriers for autistic children, even though they might rate physical activity highly and otherwise enjoy PE. Indeed, PE risks becoming an aspect of the school curriculum from which autistic children are increasingly excluded, especially if imaginative ways are not found to facilitate their participation. In 2013, for example, the DfE found that children with SEND take part in less physical activity than their peers, and that schools with the lowest levels of participation in PE had a relatively high proportion of pupils with SEND (p.14). Yet research evidence shows that all children can benefit physically and emotionally from regular exercise (Trudeau and Shephard 2008).

Conclusion

In this chapter, we have seen again how many different factors can impact on how and why autistic children learn – or don't learn – in school, and the extent to which their access to some curriculum subjects can be helped or hindered. Even when they access certain subjects, it could be the case that their ways of processing and interpreting information are at odds with general expectations.

Phonics and Writing are revealed as being frequently difficult for autistic children, underscoring the fact that some fundamental shifts are required in these subjects in order to be more broadly inclusive. Indeed, as far as Phonics is concerned, perhaps autistic children should be supported in learning how to read via alternative methods. Meanwhile, although my findings for Reading, Maths and PE are more mixed, numerous factors emerged that indicate how autistic children could more readily show their aptitudes and motivations in these areas.

Key points

- If an autistic child is not coping with Phonics, consider alternative methods of teaching Reading.

- Consider the range of reading materials available and support the reading of fact as well as fiction. Be aware that autistic children might use unanticipated information when making inferences.

- Do not rule out the use of physical items and equipment in Maths, even at a relatively advanced stage. Ensure that pupils with very high ability receive appropriate input.

- Explore sensory approaches to teaching handwriting for older children.

- Be aware that open, imaginative exercises do not suit all children.

- Try to remove social and sensory barriers to participation in PE. Team games are not for everyone.

Chapter 7

Classroom Support

Introduction

There are many different models of support for autistic children in schools, such as therapeutic and behavioural interventions (Crosland and Dunlap 2012; Drahota *et al.* 2010) delivered by visiting professionals, and structural inputs in the form of a differentiated curriculum or an alternative timetable. Specific tools and materials might also be employed (Jones *et al.* 2008), as well as TAs to provide various forms of organisational and curricular input (Cremin, Thomas and Vincett 2005). Indeed, in my experience, it's not unusual for autistic children to have a combination of all of these approaches.

Nevertheless, although a range of internal and external staff, and perhaps even peers (Chan *et al.* 2009), can be involved in the support provided to autistic children, assistance in UK schools is often provided by a TA or learning support assistant (LSA) (Dockrell *et al.* 2012), as was the case in my own study. Therefore, in this chapter, while the input of other staff members features occasionally, I focus mainly on the complex role of TAs and how their presence impacts on the social and academic progress of the children. I discuss examples of positive and not so positive support, and reflect on the circumstances in which these different conditions arise. I also consider whether or not autistic children receive input when they need it most, and touch briefly on my findings in relation to 'expertise'. When all is said and done, who are the 'experts' in autism?

The teaching assistant as teacher

What was striking in my study was that some of the autistic children had very little interaction with the class teacher and spent most of their time with the TA. Indeed, during interviews, the TAs often referred to themselves as 'the teacher' and their activity as 'teaching', and in a number of instances the TA was expected to devise both the content and learning techniques for the children they were supporting. Humphrey and Lewis (2008, p.39) found similarly that the presence of TAs resulted in 'little or no actual interaction with class teachers', a point also highlighted in Norwich and Kelly (2004). For Dockrell et al. (2012, p.18), autistic pupils were 'significantly more likely' to be working with a TA in the classroom (or to be working outside the classroom) than pupils with language impairments. Sharples, Webster and Blatchford (2015, p.4) also highlighted the ways in which 'schools have drifted into a situation in which TAs are used as an informal instructional resource for pupils with most need', and recommend that teachers divide their time equally between all pupils. In addition, and as my study substantiated, the tendency to assign responsibility for the education of the autistic children to the TA means that for teachers, it is implicit that the child is 'not within their range of responsibilities' (Emam and Farrell 2009, p.416).

Lindsay (2007, p.14) asks whether the TA should 'support, supplement, extend or replace the teacher', and cites Broer, Doyle and Giangreco (2005), who found that the TA has four potential roles: mother, friend, protector and primary teacher. In these descriptions, the role of TAs is potentially extensive, incorporating responsibilities far beyond their job description, remuneration and possibly capabilities. Indeed, for Allan (2008, p.22), TAs are 'spread so thinly across the school that there is little impact' and they 'can never give enough and are offered scant guidance on their uphill struggle'. Cremin et al. (2005, p.415) also argue that not enough attention is paid to 'the changes that might occur when these extra people move into the domain of the teacher'.

One of the consequences of this state of affairs in my own research was that the TA who, unlike the class teacher, did not benefit from paid preparation time, would clearly be making something up on the spot for the autistic child in order to give the appearance of a differentiated curriculum activity. This was evidently unsatisfactory for the child, but also for the TA, whose role should be to carry out instructions from the teacher, rather than to assume that role (Sharples *et al.* 2015). Moreover, research suggests that it is teachers who are the lynchpin to effective educational inclusion (Jones *et al.* 2008), and I observed that the children in my cohort clearly appreciated attention from the class teacher when it was given, and benefited from their pedagogical experience, training and skills.

Extra duties

As if being expected to take on the role of teacher was not enough, a number of the TAs in my study were also tasked with helping other children and running intervention activities. In the classroom, they were frequently interrupted by demands from other children, or the teacher would ask them to take a small group of children, each with diverse needs, to another location to do some focused work. This meant that the TAs were expected to use the one-to-one support the autistic child had been allocated to run small teaching groups, juggling their responsibilities to that child with trying to address the learning needs of the other children in the group. Given these circumstances, it is hardly surprising that their input to the autistic children was sometimes less than optimal, as will be seen later in this chapter. Furthermore, it's worth considering if it is equitable to expect TAs, usually at the lower end of the pay scale and not necessarily even paid in the school holidays, to carry the extent of responsibility they often do for certain children in school (Sharples *et al.* 2015).

But this does not mean the teacher was at fault either, because it was also clear, in some instances at least, that the class teacher was expected to provide a very high level of differentiation in classes containing children of a range of abilities (Bearne 1996), from diverse, multi-cultural backgrounds (Humphrey *et al.* 2006). Most lessons for the core subjects of Maths and Literacy, for example, involved the children being divided into groups according to ability, meaning that the teacher had to produce an array of learning materials and targets, which were different for each group. As a result, both the TAs and the teachers were very stretched, making it difficult for them to find time to focus meaningfully on the input for the autistic children, often falling back on to set ideas about what the autistic children might need, regardless of their individual dispositions. While diversity can be highly enriching to a school community (Humphrey *et al.* 2006), it does require particular skills and resources to ensure that the needs of all are met, and their strengths encouraged and developed.

Impact on progress

Given the multiplicity of roles TAs are expected to fulfil, we should also consider how this might impact on the progress of autistic pupils: academically, socially and even emotionally (Wittemeyer *et al.* 2011b). Certainly, the staff in my study provided numerous reasons as to why autistic children needed adult support, such as to help keep them on task and access the curriculum. The TAs were particularly inclined to see their role as helping the child in relation to behavioural problems, and some considered that they provided emotional support, or input with physical actions such as getting changed for PE. They also said that they helped the autistic children with self-organisation and to develop their independence. However, according to Cremin *et al.* (2005), studies show little by way of clear effects of TA support on pupil attainment. Meanwhile, Cigman (2007, p.28) considers the situation in starker terms, stating that 'providing a one-to-one teaching assistant is usually of no help at all' to autistic children.

In addition, if some TAs are expected to share their support amongst other children, those dedicated to a single child might unwittingly create difficulties too. Millar *et al.* (2002, p.11) raise the issue of a TA being 'velcroed' to the child, while Liasidou (2012, p.26) also discusses 'the velcro model' of TA support. For Liasidou (2012, p.26), 'the constant presence and attention of a teaching aide' means that 'disabled students are isolated and socially marginalised from their peers'. Humphrey and Lewis (2008) also found that autistic pupils considered the presence of support staff served to underscore their differences from their peers, and so prevented their integration with the rest of the class. These issues were similarly emphasised in the newspaper article entitled 'We end up hindering the pupils we're meant to help', where a teaching assistant asserted that 'too often, TAs can fall into the trap of becoming surrogate friends for vulnerable young people, who then become ostracised from their peers as a result' (The Secret Teacher 2016). These problems, the writer considers, 'can go against the core principles of inclusive education and segregate those with SEND from other students' (The Secret Teacher 2016).

In addition, Wittemeyer *et al.* (2011b) express concerns that, due to the perpetual presence of TAs, autistic children – unlike other children – are not allowed to make mistakes because they are constantly being corrected. I also found that because of this phenomenon, the autistic children were being denied 'zoning out' time, despite the fact that mind-wandering can enable creative problem-solving, for example (Mooneyham and Schooler 2013). What is evident, therefore, is that while teachers 'rely heavily' on TAs (Emam and Farrell 2009, p.407), their role and effectiveness are unclear, and they might even be hindering the educational progress, social integration and emotional well-being of some pupils. In other words, if TAs are not appropriately deployed, they can become the unwitting drivers of exclusion, rather than the facilitators of inclusion.

Effective support

Some of the parents in my study welcomed the support the TAs provided and spoke in fulsome terms of how much they valued their input, especially if they showed an emotional commitment to the role and had developed a relationship of trust with their child. Similarly, a number of the children in my study appreciated the support of the TAs and liked being able to speak confidentially to them about issues of concern, for example. A couple of the autistic adults also said that they wished they had had this kind of emotional support from a TA when they were at school. These points are highly instructive, because they contrast with the more practical or technical comments of school staff in relation to the reasons why additional support was required, although some of the TAs also spoke about their support in emotional terms, and were keen to point out how fond they were of the children.

In Juniors – we were eventually able to have a couple of quite good TAs – their job was to be with me, in or out of the class. They did a very good job, because they took the time to get to know me. (George)

▓ Pre-tutoring was very helpful to me in primary school because the timetable stuck up on the wall with different cards showing what lessons we were going to do that day was pretty much useless. It showed me what lesson, but not what we were going to do in the lesson, so the teaching assistant or the teacher themselves telling me what we were going to do before the lesson starts was great because then I could mentally prepare for what we were going to do and start thinking about what answers I might give or how I might respond to the task given. (Grace, 14)

▓ (I had) 8 hours a week of 1:1 support. Proved very helpful and consisted of training with social skills, idioms and other eccentricities of the English language. (Michael)

Furthermore, in Chapter 5 I discussed how the intense interests of autistic children can be positively harnessed in school (Gunn and Delafield-Butt 2016), and that this phenomenon also played a crucial role in terms of the effectiveness of adult support. For example, when the autistic children were engaged in an activity that was intrinsically motivating to them, the need for constant reminders evaporated. The children were more relaxed, focused and independent in these circumstances, and so the staff were more able to support them in an enabling and constructive way. Negative reminders to concentrate and engage, and repeated instructions and pleas to tackle the job in hand, were replaced by more positive comments and encouragement. In fact, this reciprocity grew through activities, with the more constructive and skilled support from the TA meaning that the child became calmer, more attentive and responsive (Wood 2019). This also sometimes resulted in a power shift from the adult to the child, as the activities became more child-led, rather than adult-prompted. It also meant it was easier for peers to engage and, as we will see in Chapter 8, which deals with communication, some of the children were able to speak more fluently when talking about their interests too.

Ineffective support

Notwithstanding the good intentions of school staff and the positive examples of input described, the support experienced by the children, perceived by the parents and some of the autistic adults in my study, was in some cases more often negative than positive. For example, some parents complained that their child was not getting enough TA support, or even that they were receiving less input than they were entitled to (as set out, for example, in the EHC plan). In particular, parents felt that if their child was well-behaved, or was considered not to be bothering anyone, they were just left to muddle along on their own (Batten *et al.* 2006). This point was also made by some of the autistic adults in my study: if they were deemed to be coping well academically, other aspects of their time in school, which they found problematic, were ignored. In other words, support is provided negatively, in response to problems defined by others, rather than positively, in response to problems experienced by the child (Allan 2008). And so, while these points underscore the fact that TAs are highly valued, they also demonstrate that if autistic children are not creating evident difficulties for others, they might not receive the help they need.

■ Someone to translate what was expected of me – that would have made a world of difference. It was more an understanding of the expectations. I needed a social translator. Even a couple of hints every day would have saved a lot of heartache. (Jon)

In addition, some of the autistic adults particularly highlighted inflexibility (see in Chapter 1 how this is deemed to be one of the impairments associated with autism) on the part of teachers as being very problematic. I also found this to be the case, such as when school staff would insist on the autistic children carrying out certain tasks in a prescribed way, at a set time, dictated by some misguided sense that this would aid the child's independence. Indeed, school staff, quite understandably you might think, were perhaps preoccupied with the school routine and timetable, and yet it was the children who were described as being 'set in their ways', and so difficult to 'keep on task'.

Other problems were that some school staff thought that task repetition was a useful learning tool for autistic children

(Fentress and Lerman 2012), and so they were expected to carry out the same tasks, repetitively, particularly when they had been provided with especially made, differentiated materials (Wood 2019). Furthermore, instructions could be unclear or confused, and remarks occasionally insensitive, such as turning to other children and complimenting their work, or speaking about the autistic children as if they weren't present. There was also the application of rather pointless 'special needs' paraphernalia and apparatus such as 'now and next' boards, visual timetables and timers, regardless of whether or not they served any genuine educational purpose (Wood 2018a).

All of these issues resulted in the children sometimes being distracted, demotivated and non-compliant, meaning that they required a high level of prompting. Therefore, the reasons for providing support, such as the need to keep the children on task, or to control behaviour, could at least in part be explained by unimaginative and repetitive activities the children were expected to carry out. This contrasted with the much more positive dynamics which occurred when a flexible approach to the child's learning was taken, often focused on their interests (Wood 2019).

This a useful point to introduce an anecdote from Jon, although it concerns a teacher rather than a TA. Jon explains how, when he was in Year 4 and already a talented artist but with undiagnosed dyslexia, he drew a picture of a Tudor street. The head teacher saw Jon's picture and was very impressed, suggesting that it should be put on the wall of the main hall, an honour rarely bestowed to pupils. This is what happened next:

> My class teacher said to me 'write your name on it' and the subject. I knew I had a choice – either ask for help, whereupon he would ridicule me, or try to do it on my own. So I had a go on my own. I got my name wrong. When I gave it to him, the teacher held it up, said 'what a stupid boy', and tore it up, threw it in the bin. That was the reason I didn't become an artist until much later in life. (Jon)

Fortunately, the staff in my study were generally sensitive and supportive to the autistic children, and perhaps Jon's example hails from a different time when attitudes were harsher. Jon has reproduced the drawing of the Tudor street, as he would have done it then, for this book:

Break times and extra-curricular activities

One of the consequences of TAs often only being paid for the specific hours they spend with the autistic children is that they may consequently have no support at all when it is most needed: during break and lunchtimes (Humphrey and Symes 2011; Sainsbury 2009). It can also mean, as we have already seen, that autistic children don't get to take part in before- and after-school clubs, or go on school trips (Batten *et al.* 2006).

Moreover, if the one-to-one support the children receive is diluted by the TA being required to support other children at the same time, or other children have a TA 'velcroed' to them (Liasidou 2012) in class, the potential absence of TA input during break times is even more problematic. Already a difficult time of the school day for some autistic children due to their unstructured and socially complex nature, break times also present opportunities for bullies, as the autistic adults in my study, in particular, recounted.

> I found them completely unstructured with not a lot to do. I didn't enjoy it. Breaks are meant to be breaks, they're meant to be time off, but when there's nothing to do and no one to talk to, it's not really a break. (George)

> The library, where I spend almost all of my break/lunchtimes, is often busy and loud because of boys in older year groups misbehaving and causing a lot of trouble. The queues in the canteen at lunch are huge and it takes ages to get my food and I am very claustrophobic, so the crowds can be stressful to me. (Grace, 14)

> Break time was not a break. I'd be teased mercilessly. (Jon)

> I got through it; the unstructured time is not suited to autistic people at all. (Michael)

Nevertheless, my contributors James (aged 8) and Zack (aged 10) both said that they enjoyed break times because they got to play football with their friends, while Rose had more mixed feelings about these times of the day:

> I hate it when we're the last year to eat; it hurts your tummy and I hate it. If you're last sitting, you're the last people to have your lunch. You can be waiting in a very long queue just to get your food, and your tummy hurts, and that happens to me every day. Otherwise – I enjoy breaks and lunchtimes. The best time is free time so you can just sleep throughout the entire thing if you want to. You can daydream so much – it is really fun to actually dream and sleep

throughout the whole of break time. Most of the time I dream about how amazing I can be when I grow up, how famous I can be, things like that. Sometimes I get up and run around with my friends. (Rose, 8)

Autism and expertise

School staff and some parents in my research study stated on occasions that they felt they were not 'experts' in autism, and hoped that qualified professionals, such as speech and language therapists, or that some sort of 'autism training', might somehow provide the key to the educational inclusion of the autistic children. 'Expertise' lay elsewhere, they said, as they were not 'specialists', sometimes causing them to doubt their own natural, and arguably more humane, instincts.

In fact, there was no particular evidence in my study that school staff who had received training in autism were more adept than those who had not. Some of the most sensitive and thoughtful input was provided by teachers and TAs who had received no training at all, and who had not, to their knowledge, worked with an autistic child before.

> We had a different teacher for Maths. She understood autism, it seemed. She was able to know what to do, and because of it, it made the classroom experience enjoyable. The staff who liked me, liked me because they got to know me, and not the disability. (George)

Meanwhile, some examples of poor support came from school staff who were 'trained in autism' and consisted of a perfunctory delivery of strategies and techniques they had been told autistic children required (Allan 2008). Such misconceptions were predicated on the idea that the children were 'different', somehow 'other', whereby the child is considered to fall outside the realms of the knowledge and experiences of typical school staff (Davis *et al.* 2000).

Indeed, Allan (2010, p.609) critiques the inclusive training manuals which offer 'strategies for managing difference', while for Thomas (2012, p.477), the 'relentlessly deficit-oriented history of special education' has done little to further inclusive practices. Therefore, while training in autism can, of course, be useful, it is important that this does not lead school staff to perceive the autistic children as 'strangers' (Slee and Allan 2001), causing them to set aside more instinctive and natural forms of engagement. My findings suggest that valuing the children according to their particular dispositions, demonstrating a genuine commitment to their well-being, learning and progress, will be ultimately much more valuable than the strategies and techniques doled out in training programmes or in books. Indeed, while training in autism can be beneficial, the real experts will usually be the autistic children and adults themselves (Milton 2014b).

Conclusion

Support in school for autistic children can be provided in a range of ways, but a dedicated TA is often the primary source of additional aid. However, TAs can be expected to carry a level of responsibility for the children far in excess of their allotted duties, a situation that is potentially difficult for them, and far from ideal for the children. Not only does this mean that the autistic children are not receiving sufficient input from the person qualified to educate them – the class teacher – but they are potentially perceived as somehow separate from the rest of the class, and so 'othered'. However, this situation is not usually the fault of the teachers, who are often very stretched themselves.

In addition, some autistic children have the opposite problem – that the TA is 'velcroed' to them – creating barriers to their socialisation and denying them the opportunity to make mistakes or to simply 'zone out'. Meanwhile, autistic children may well be denied support at the times of the day when they need it most – during breaks and lunchtimes – and could also be excluded from school trips due to limitations of resources and staffing.

Although the school staff in my study listed a number of reasons why their support was needed in relation to the autistic children, it was often the less tangible, more emotional aspects of support that was valued by them. Furthermore, this support was much more likely to be effective when the children were able to focus on their interests, while inflexibility, task repetition and excessive prompting were especially detrimental to their learning and well-being.

Ultimately however, the important question does not concern the inherent abilities or lack thereof of school staff, but rather to consider what the circumstances are in which they are more likely to be able to demonstrate skill and to be effective in their support. Indeed, my research showed that the quality of support provided by TAs could vary greatly according to different circumstances, and that examples of ineffective and sometimes counter-productive support, as well as highly effective support, could be provided by the very same person, with the same child.

Key points

- It is essential to take a holistic view of the support given to an autistic child, and to see TAs as part of an overall framework of assistance, rather than the sole providers of input.

- The TA should not, in most circumstances, be expected to take on the role of the child's teacher. Nor should the TA be overburdened with responsibilities for other children.

- At the same time, the TA should not be 'velcroed' to the child.

- Support should be provided when the child most needs it, and must not be limited by considerations around staffing.

- The effectiveness of support should always be critically evaluated from the perspective of the child, rather than the requirements of the adults.

- Training in autism can be useful, but school staff should not ignore their own instincts or set aside more natural forms of meaningful engagement in the name of 'autism strategies'.

Chapter 8

Communication

Introduction

It wouldn't be hard to argue that being able to communicate and to be understood by others is fundamental to our sense of well-being, belonging, participation and inclusion in society. By contrast, not being able to express our needs, thoughts and wishes, or not being understood when we are trying to do so, is the very definition, it seems to me, of alienation and exclusion. Indeed, it is for these reasons that the right to communicate is enshrined in national and international laws and conventions (CRPD; UN DESA 2006), as will be summarised in this chapter.

■ Communication as a human right is ignored, people don't try because they don't have to, they aren't expected to. Why is this acceptable? Why isn't supported decision-making the 'go to', why are our rights lesser than others? (Kabie)

At the same time, readers will be aware that many autistic children are considered to have communication difficulties (APA 2013), and schools often place a strong emphasis on speech and language supports and interventions as a result (Roulstone *et al.* 2012). And so in this chapter, I discuss briefly what those difficulties are deemed to be, and consider the complex issues raised when children are thought to be poor communicators. When all is said and done, are we really 'listening' to those children, or are we instead simply paying attention to what we want to hear?

In addition, I describe the impact of the context within which autistic children are expected to communicate in school and explore the different ways autistic children might choose to express themselves. Ultimately, should we be thinking differently, and better, about their communication?

The legal argument

To start with, the requirement to support all children to communicate effectively is enshrined in international conventions and national laws. According to the UNCRC (UNICEF 1989), for example, children have the right to express their views 'freely in all matters affecting the child' (Article 12), and, as we have seen, information should be imparted or expressed through any medium that the child chooses. This underscores the point that the emphasis should not always be placed on speech, and that children have the right to be supported in expressing themselves in the ways that most suit them. However, as you will see later in this chapter, my own study shows that this is not always the case.

The CRPD (UN DESA 2006) explicitly extends the right to communicate – which should be 'on an equal basis with other children' (Article 7) – to disabled children too, stipulating that they should be 'provided with disability and age-appropriate assistance to realize that right' (Article 7). Similarly, and within a national context, the CFA (2014), asserts that 'the wishes of...the young person' (Section 33) should be taken into account, and that local authorities must have regard to 'the importance of the child and his or her parent, or the young person, participating as fully as possible in decisions relating to the exercise of the function concerned' (Section 19).

Therefore, both international and national legislation are clear that the views of disabled children must be sought in a manner that enables them to express themselves as easily as possible. Indeed, according to the CRPD (UN DESA 2006), such measures are necessary to enable 'full inclusion' (Article 24) in society.

Communication difficulties

As discussed in Chapter 1, a diagnosis of autism usually involves the identification of some element of communication difficulty, or 'language abnormalities' (Wing and Gould 1979, p.11). These are considered to include a range of problems, including understanding (Bartak, Rutter and Cox 1975), narrative delivery (Norbury and Bishop 2003), use of pronouns (Lee, Hobson and Chiat 1994) and intonation (Tager-Flusberg, Rhea and Lord 2005), amongst many other issues (Rapin and Dunn 2013). 'Selective mutism' – an ability to communicate in some situations but not in others – has also been associated with autism (McKenna *et al.* 2017).

Diagnostic manuals like the DSM-5 (APA 2013) refer to 'persistent deficits in social communication and social interaction',[1] where the emphasis is more on the social and interactive nature of communication. In addition, autistic children may be classified, somewhat simplistically, according to whether they are 'verbal' or 'non-verbal', with those considered to be 'non-verbal' associated with low attainment in school (Dockrell *et al.* 2012) and poor longer-term outcomes (Howlin, Mawhood and Rutter 2000). Interestingly, in the ICD-11 (WHO 2018), an important diagnostic manual, it is stated that autistic people can exhibit 'a full range' of language skill, although the measure of this ability pivots on the notion of 'functional language', a problematic concept given that what is thought to be functional for one person, might not be for another.

■ I consider that I used to have communication difficulties – pronouncing certain words such as 'hospital' and 'spaghetti'. If I have them now, they are very minor and don't get in the way of things. (George)

■ I can't say hard words sometimes. (James, 8)

■ I find talking difficult. (Zack, 10)

Some research has focused on how ideas are conveyed and what autistic people choose to talk about (Loveland *et al.* 1990). Dean, Fox Adams and Kasari (2013, pp.151–152) noted that an autistic girl is rejected by her peers because of her 'narrative delivery', the 'idiosyncratic/repetitive nature of her stories, and her persistence despite receiving peer sanctioning'. In this account, the autistic girl continues to narrate certain events, despite her 'peers' (a group of

---

1   See www.cdc.gov/ncbddd/autism/hcp-dsm.html

girls she has been placed with for the purposes of the research) seemingly making it clear that they are not interested in what she has to say. The researchers conclude that the problem lies with the girl and the fact that she is autistic, not with the other members of the group, one of whom, the authors note, fails to maintain the attention of the others, but nevertheless emerges as their leader.

Thus, language impairment in autistic people is considered to include potentially multiple deficits, including their understanding, linguistic development, the topics they choose to talk about and how they communicate and engage in social situations, as summarised by the following:

> Many questions remain to be answered about communication in autism. For example, how is odd intonation related to deficits in communication and social cognition? How do linguistic comprehension deficits relate to the various aspects of deviant language seen in the syndrome? What triggers the initial failure of social cognition and joint attention that seems to be associated with such pervasive communicative difficulties? (Tager-Flusberg *et al.* 2005, p.356)

Indeed, while some autistic people are deemed impaired because they are 'non-verbal', those who are 'verbal' might similarly be viewed as dysfunctional due to apparently saying the wrong things, in the wrong way and at the wrong time (Wood 2018a).

Understanding and belief

Being classified as having communication impairments can lead to the assumption that the person is intellectually disabled too, and that any utterances might be irrelevant or nonsensical, and so not to be taken seriously. Wing (2007, p.28) asserts a number of times that the 'understanding' of autistic children is often lower than their speech suggests, stating similarly that some 'may appear to have some pretend play', but that this is, in fact, 'an empty copy of other children's play'. We also saw in Chapter 6 that autistic children's reading can be seen as a fairly superficial process, devoid of genuine understanding. Consequently, these viewpoints suggest that autistic children might speak, play and read, but that true comprehension and meaningful engagement are absent.

In addition, it is often assumed that autistic people 'who are considered minimally verbal or nonverbal' are 'the most cognitively impaired' (Dawson *et al.* 2007, p.657). Lawson (2008, p.80) also challenges the notion that autistic people who 'don't talk' must be 'intellectually disabled':

> ...language is considered the traditional normal currency of communication. Therefore, if you don't use language as your communication tool, you may be considered disabled, disordered or dysfunctional. (Lawson 2008, p.74)

Moreover, Davis *et al.* (2000) found that staff in a special school questioned the ability of some children to be able to express themselves, which in turn impaired the efforts to communicate of those children. Therefore, if communication impairments are unquestioningly considered to be a core feature of autism, this can also lead to a tendency to neither trust nor value the communication of autistic people.

I didn't speak much in infant school. I was able to speak but I had periods of time where I couldn't. This was usually when I was under great stress, for example when the teacher was talking directly to me. There was an incident where another child bit me quite badly – I didn't bother telling anyone because I don't think I saw the point. My mother saw it and got cross, she took me to school and demanded to see the teacher/head teacher. So I had three people looking at me, talking at me, interrogating me. I just shut down, I don't recall anyone actually asking me to show them the bite; they were just pulling at my clothes and invading my space and overloading me. When we got home my mother was so cross, she decided that I'd wilfully 'shown her up' and that the school thought that she was lying. She still mentioned this 30 years later as an example of what a bad child I was! (Kabie)

These issues arguably reach their zenith in debates about Facilitated Communication (FC), which was originally devised by Rosemary Crossley to help people who have difficulties with the physical act of communicating, rather than the cognitive processes required. FC involves support being provided to someone who has limited or no speech, as well as motor control or planning difficulties, to point to letters on a board or grid in order to spell out words. More recently, FC has been used to help autistic people to communicate, but has consistently failed tests of validity on the question of authorship when subjected to scientific scrutiny (Schlosser *et al.* 2014). Indeed, studies show that the person facilitating the communication is the real 'author' of the words typed by the disabled individual (Jacobson, Mulick and Schwartz 1995). So, by extension, any external help provided to a disabled person to be able to communicate can be viewed with suspicion.

However, in a fascinating article, Erevelles (2002) asserts that the discrediting of FC is based on an assumption that typically, any of us are able to represent ourselves fully through language, without any sort of problem or ambiguity. Which, when you think about the sorts of misunderstandings we all experience on a daily basis, is a very good point. Furthermore, Erevelles (2002) argues that while autistic people are perceived as disordered and irrational, the very techniques used to test the validity of FC are predicated on notions of order and reason, qualities autistic people are considered to lack. Therefore, while FC as an authentic means of communication is highly contested, including within the autistic community where it has been associated by some with abuse (Hearst 2016), questions remain about how its validity has been assessed. Indeed, for the autistic writer Klar-Wolfond (2008, p.115), a key issue is the requirement to 'base everything on our need for proof of either competence or incompetence'.

A further important example within the debate of validity when non-verbal forms of communication are used is provided by the autistic activist Amanda Baggs (2006). Her video 'In My Language' which, at the time of writing, has reached 1.4 million views on YouTube, shows her humming, tapping, flicking and rocking, which she describes as 'my native language'. She 'translates' these physical responses by typing and using voice output software, which she employs apparently unaided. Baggs (2006) explains how the way she thinks and responds to her environment is 'so different from standard concepts or even visualization that some people do not consider it thought at all'. Similarly, she describes how she is considered impaired because she struggles with the language of others, who are not correspondingly thought to lack ability even though they do not understand her language. However, and perhaps somewhat consistently with the issues relating to belief and credibility previously described, Baggs has a number of detractors, some of whom describe her as a 'fraud' (Amanda Baggs Autism Controversy 2009). Interestingly, no such controversy appears to have accompanied the publication of two highly popular books by Higashida (2014, 2017), despite the fact that both were written via facilitated methods.

Role of support

We saw in the last chapter how the support the autistic children received played a crucial role in various aspects of their participation, inclusion and well-being in school. This support was also very important in relation to their communication.

Fortunately, some school staff helped the children in a positive and enabling fashion, avoiding any kind of pressure or stress, and presenting them with genuine choices. These staff showed flexibility and humour, and demonstrated a sincere desire to enable the children to express themselves in an unadulterated manner (Wood 2018a). Furthermore, as we saw in Chapter 5, just as the support skills of school staff were observed to be enhanced when the children were engaged in motivating activities (Wood 2019), their ability to interact and encourage the children's communication improved in these circumstances too. And so this underscores the point that communication is a two-way reciprocal act (Muskett 2016; Wood and Milton 2018), where the right kind of input not only helps children to express themselves, but also correspondingly impacts positively on the communication of the supporting adult.

Teachers need to understand that they need to attend to us and be ready for subtle forms of communication, that stress, or excitement, fear, overload, etc., etc. will make us communicate differently. They need to learn to actively listen and learn about us as individuals. Communication is two-way and they may have to work to really hear us. We may not use the right tone of voice or body language, but our words still need to be heard. (Kabie)

However, there were also difficulties in this area. I have described already how poorly planned (or completely unplanned) activities presented under the banner of 'differentiation' could be profoundly demotivating and counter-productive. I also noticed, in some cases, how this appeared to have a deleterious effect on the child's spoken communication, as the child became weary and demoralised. In addition, some of the children were not native speakers of English, but any difficulties they experienced with spoken and written communication, or understanding, were deemed to stem from being autistic, rather than the fact that they were not fully bilingual.

Moreover, while some staff demonstrated a high level of proficiency in supporting the communication of the autistic children, others were not necessarily skilled communicators themselves: instructions were vague, confusing or even contradictory at times. And yet no one questioned the effectiveness of their support in terms of the communication skills of the autistic children, whose difficulties were deemed to stem from the very fact of being autistic alone, rather than any other factors entirely unrelated to them.

> Effective communication with autistic people is about trying to see things from their point of view. Make sure your language is clear and unambiguous and that they're not distracted (if possible!). If this proves difficult, pressuring them to talk to you at that very moment in time could be counterproductive – in extreme cases this could potentially even induce meltdowns due to pre-existing stress levels. (Michael)

Another issue was that sometimes, support for the communication of the autistic children slipped into control of their communication, both in terms of what the children expressed and how they did so (Wood 2018a). For example, one child was provided with a 'choosing board', ostensibly to help his communication and independence. However, the amount of actual 'choice' this child was provided with was negligible, because if he 'chose' an activity that the adult didn't want him to do, he would be made to select another card. Or he would be removed from a task he was already enjoying to 'choose' a picture representing it from the board, provoking anxiety on his part that he was being removed from his preferred activity.

Therefore, some of the children were simply ignored if they were communicating something different from what the adult had in mind, or they would be made to express themselves in ways that didn't really work for them. Indeed, the Children's Commissioner, with reference to the UNCRC (UNICEF 1989), asked 'are we listening, and if we are, are we acting on what we hear?' (Atkinson, foreword in Pellicano *et al.* 2014, p.3).

In addition, two of the children in my study were described as 'non-verbal', and yet I often heard them say words, either when they were objecting to a certain task, or when they were engaged in an activity of interest. Sadly, these words were uttered into a void, neither heard nor acknowledged by the supporting staff, who might instead be preoccupied with some sort of communication paraphernalia, such as a visual timetable, or a 'now and next' board. Or the staff member might be verbally labelling items and actions, regardless of whether or not this involved any real engagement with the child. Indeed, sometimes staff seemed to be going through the motions of communication support, but without actually responding to and interacting with the child. Moreover, and especially with the younger children, there was a concern that they should learn social niceties (Bottema-Beutel, Park and Kim 2018), such as greeting the class teacher in the morning, rather than focusing on what mattered to the child.

In these instances, the support for communication that the school provided sometimes proved both contradictory and demotivating, where the child gained as little from trying to communicate as from failing to interact at all. Here, the emphasis was on compliance, rather than supporting the child's communication needs. Moreover, while it was evident that the children were more skilled communicators than the adults appeared to realise in some cases, the combined labels of 'autism' and 'non-verbal' resulted in the children not being heard, or their wishes not being respected. Indeed, to label a child with communication difficulties can mean paradoxically that adults cease to observe, listen to and engage with that child. However, examples of good practice were certainly evident, and so it is vital that support staff are provided with the time and space they need to be able to develop these skills and share them with others (Wood 2018a).

Communication context

My argument is not that autistic children are devoid of communication difficulties, but rather that unthinking assumptions can paradoxically make it much harder for them to make themselves understood. In fact, all of the 10 autistic children in my study, to a greater or lesser extent, experienced problems with spoken communication. According to their parents, they either did not have any speech at all, or language had been slow to develop in comparison to their peers (Mitchell *et al.* 2006). School staff also commented that some of the autistic children struggled to put their thoughts into words. Indeed, although none of the children was, in fact, 'non-verbal', some did have a very limited vocabulary, and mispronunciation of words and difficulty of recall were common (Norbury *et al.* 2010). Anecdotes could also be jumbled, both in terms of the words used and the order of events (Miniscalco *et al.* 2007). And so the autistic children certainly demonstrated some of the speech and language difficulties I outlined earlier.

However, it was also clear that the context within which the children were expected to communicate could have a significant impact on their ability to make themselves understood. We have already seen the damaging effects of noise, for example, and the complex circumstances in which an autistic child might be expected to concentrate and work (Sainsbury 2009). Indeed, research has shown that noise, including background chatter, can have a particularly damaging impact on pupils with SEND, making language processing and learning more difficult (Dockrell and Shield 2006; Klatte *et al.* 2013). Yet the children in my study who were seated with a TA in a corridor, for example, or to one side of the classroom while the rest of the children were noisily engaged in another activity, were having to deal with more noise and disruption than their peers. Therefore, while the children demonstrated difficulties with speech, these problems could be compounded by the challenging circumstances within which they were expected to communicate.

> If I am very stressed, my ability to communicate will break down. (George)

If it's a close friend, then talking is easy and I generally like it, but not-so-close friends and teachers/staff/other students can be difficult because (at secondary school in particular) a lot of the girls in my year will judge me and talk about me behind my back so I have to be careful what I say. Talking to teachers is awkward sometimes as I can't be quite as honest as I would with my close friends because I would hate to offend them by saying something negative about the subject they teach, and I always make an effort to keep a positive relationship with my teachers. It helps if all of my teachers know that I am terrified of speaking in front of the class. (Grace, 14)

Sometimes I self-mute, sometimes I cannot get the words out of myself, if I'm in a situation which is hostile. If I am calm I can comment. (Jon)

When I'm stressed I can lose the ability to talk fluently. For example, when I went through airport security with my phone in my pocket and caused the alarm to go off. Because I was so stressed and they were trying to get me into a body scanner all I could say (shout) was 'phone', 'bag', 'bag', 'phone'. I was trying to tell them that I'd made the alarm go off because of my phone and that my alert card was in my bag – which was on the conveyer belt thingy. All they saw was a shouty person trying to push through security shouting and trying to get past. Also I may just stop talking. Or I will just start agreeing to everything to make people go away. (Kabie)

Nevertheless, other circumstances were seen to have a much more positive impact, and so we must return again to the subject of intense interests. For example, if the children struggled with open questions at times, this format seemed much more manageable when they were talking about subjects that interested them. Verbal responses in these situations were generally longer, more fluent and readily provided, and the children were more relaxed.

One child, for example, who was often hesitant and struggled to answer most of my interview questions, was absolutely transformed when she was talking about a book she was enjoying. Here, she employed a wider lexis, a more varied sentence structure, asked questions, made comments and provided explanations

(Wood 2019). She also related aspects of the book to other events in her life, read independently and sought out information from different pages, showing higher-level reading skills identified by the DfE (2015c) as being linked to positive longer-term health, educational and employment outcomes. Above all, this child was the dominant communication partner in her exchanges with the TA, initiating the discussion, directing the conversation and even feeling sufficiently confident to correct the TA on one occasion (Wood 2019). Interestingly, this activity took place in quite a noisy classroom, which suggests that the drawbacks of noise might be counterbalanced by the advantages of intense interests.

Therefore, enabling autistic children to focus on areas that interest them could have a significant, positive influence on how they express themselves, also resulting in an important shift in the power dynamic, with the child taking a more confident and assertive role in communication exchanges. In these circumstances, which I also found led to more, not less, compliance from the child, the communication needs of the child are supported and valued, rather than the intentions of the adult in charge.

Non-verbal communication

We all express ourselves in a myriad of non-verbal ways (Mehrabian and Ferris 1967), and autistic children are no exception to this. One boy in my study, who was not a native speaker of English, often struggled to find his words, but was able to employ a range of gestures, actions and mimes as he related what he was interested in. Another child would place the hand of his TA on a closed book to indicate he had had enough, or put an item away to show that he wanted to do something else. And yet these important messages could be ignored or pass entirely unnoticed.

In fact, research suggests that autistic children from bilingual homes are not necessarily disadvantaged in terms of their linguistic development compared with non-autistic children, and also that they might use more gestures over time (Zhou *et al.* 2017). The employment of gesture has also been found to be an important indicator in identifying whether or not young children have communication difficulties, or instead are simply 'late talkers' (Crais, Watson and Baranek 2009).

In addition, as we saw in Chapter 2, the class teachers in my study revealed a number of strategies aimed at gaining silence in the classroom. This was despite the fact that a lot of noise was seemingly tolerated by them. However, in the drive to encourage the communication of the autistic children, I found that their silence could be overlooked.

As I explained, some of the autistic children were noted to be clearer and more fluent in their speech when talking about topics that interested them. But others were observed instead to be silent, calm and concentrated when engaged with motivating activities. One child, for example, had high levels of focus and concentration, but very little speech. However, when he was contentedly and silently absorbed in activities that interested him, evoking the 'flow states' (McDonnell and Milton 2014) described in Chapter 5, he was sometimes interrupted by the communication interventions intended to help him. If he was engrossed in looking at a book, his well-intentioned TA might try to get him to label the pictures, meaning that his 'silent communication' was not recognised and was, in fact, disrupted by attempts to help him communicate.

However, according to Davis *et al.* (2000, p.210), children must be permitted to be 'the final gatekeepers to their worlds' and have the right to not respond if they so wish. This point is also made by Lewis (2010, p.20), who considers that 'listening better includes hearing silence' and recognising that 'silence is not neutral or empty'. Acheson (2008) has also argued that silence must be understood within the specific, intersubjective contexts where it is manifested. Therefore, in the drive to help autistic children to communicate, we must not ignore the expressive value of their silence and other forms of non-spoken communication.

■ Right now, we still have people saying that some autistic people 'do not communicate at all' – there isn't any real understanding of how to assist people. (Kabie)

Communication differences

The autistic adults in my study offered some interesting perspectives on the issue of silence, as well as communication more generally. They complained, for example, that non-autistic people seem to feel the need to 'fill silences' and to talk for the sake of it, without having anything meaningful to say. Indeed, they commented on what they considered to be the propensity of non-autistic people to engage in pointless chit-chat, which was felt to be a waste of time. According to them, the meanings of non-autistic people might also be unclear, inaccurate and buried in useless verbiage, without them even getting to the point of what they actually want to say.

■ The difficulties I encounter are due to others not understanding or not being willing to understand or not explain things properly. (George)

■ Non-autistic people seem to have...quite rigid ways of communicating – they need to recognise and accept this. I feel that how autistic people communicate is different, sometimes obviously so: people who use text to speech software or symbols or sign; sometimes not so obviously. (Kabie)

In fact, some of the school staff valued the honesty and straightforward nature of the communication of the autistic children, which they said was refreshing. Furthermore, in interviews with the children, I sometimes found that questions were answered in a delayed, alternative, literal or tautological manner. In other words, they did answer the question, but in ways I hadn't anticipated. And as we saw in Chapter 4, this phenomenon also has implications for how autistic children perform in tests and exams. But is a literal response to a question 'wrong' or of less value than one that is more interpretive? Does a delayed response make that answer less valid? These are the sorts of questions that need to be tackled if autistic children are to be supported and valued in their communication.

Nowadays I have no difficulties in communication. When I was younger, communication was harder as people are very unclear in their language and I couldn't decode it. Things like metaphors, idioms, indirect requests, etc., which aren't to be taken literally, were often misinterpreted by me. If only people could say what they actually mean! (Michael)

These issues suggest that while some autistic children certainly have communication difficulties, especially in terms of speech, there are also matters of interpretation, of one person imposing a way of looking at the world, and responding to events, on another. Indeed, we only have to look at the ideas of philosophers of language and meaning, such as Barthes (1968), to realise that understanding is a complex interweaving of different positionalities, assumptions and perspectives. Within the context of autism, this has been framed as the 'double empathy' problem (Milton 2012a), whereby the misunderstandings between autistic and non-autistic people are not considered to derive from autistic social impairment (Heasman and Gillespie 2017), but rather, mutual misunderstandings. Indeed, despite being positioned as 'different', there is no hesitation on the part of educators and assessors, for example, in thinking they can confidently interpret the worlds of autistic children.

Communicating with non-autistic people is always a problem. Sometimes it feels as though I speak a different language! I tend to have the wrong tone of voice and look really 'flat'; for example, when in labour I just said in a matter of fact way: 'it really hurts I think I'm about to give birth', meaning that I only just got into the delivery room on time on a couple of occasions. When telling the doctor I feel depressed or that something hurts a lot I don't say it in a way that makes them believe me. In my life I've been in extreme danger but haven't been taken seriously by police, etc. because of the way I communicate. (Kabie)

Furthermore, research is beginning to shed new light on phenomena such as echolalia (a tendency to repeat words and phrases, typically considered to have little functional benefit), showing that it does, in fact, have a communicative role and can be a stepping stone to language development (Gernsbacher, Morson and Grace 2016). In addition, Gernsbacher *et al.* (2016) question the generally held view that for autistic children, there is a gap between receptive and expressive language development, and that pronoun misuse, for example, is unique to autism. So, while some autistic children do require help with their communication, there is also a need to recognise that sometimes they are simply communicating differently, and so it is incumbent on supporting adults to recognise and value their modes of expression.

Conclusion

The right to communicate, and to be supported in so-doing, is enshrined in law. And good support can enable autistic children to develop self-confidence, independence and agency. However, the very identification of speech and language difficulties in children can mean that adults are oblivious to the various ways the children express themselves, or even that they disbelieve them entirely. Moreover, helping children to communicate can slip into controlling their self-expression, rather than valuing what matters to them. As a result, poor support in this area can be disempowering and achieve the opposite of the desired intentions of independence and improved communication.

In addition, the situations within which autistic children are expected to express themselves can have a very major impact, both positively and negatively. And even though autistic children might have some difficulties with speech in particular, they are not necessarily poor communicators, and may express themselves in a myriad of unrecognised ways. Furthermore, it is worth considering whether in some cases at least, the issue is not so much of communication difficulties, but communication differences (Heasman and Gillespie 2018).

One member of staff had commented that autistic people are unable to read non-verbal clues, but my evidence indicates that part of the problem, at least, lies with the inability of non-autistic people to understand the sometimes very evident verbal and non-verbal communication of autistic children and adults. Therefore, it is essential to recognise and support the range of ways in which autistic children might be communicating and to adopt a multi-modal approach to communication support. This could also include computers and other technological devices (Murray and Lawson 2007), which appear to be somewhat underused in terms of communication support in schools (Wood 2018a).

> Communication is the MOST important thing and learning how to say no and express thoughts in a way that can be understood – whatever that is: not just verbally (verbal expression shouldn't be seen as the ultimate as it is now; it's communication to be understood that matters). (Kabie)

Key points

- Good support consists of valuing what the child wants to communicate and how the child wants to do so. Adults should be sensitive and responsive to the different ways in which autistic children communicate.

- Noisy, busy environments, where there is a lot of background chatter, can make it more difficult for autistic children to communicate effectively.

- Enabling autistic children to focus on their interests can have a positive impact on their ability to communicate.

- Communication can be silent and this should not necessarily be problematised.

- The interactive, shared nature of communication should be emphasised, taking into account the style and skills of the communication partner.

- There is a need to employ more technology for communication support.

- A child's communication must be validated, even if they are not 'on message' with what the adult wants to hear.

Chapter 9

Socialisation

Teachers should know that friendship isn't always that easy – sometimes when you make a friend, they can be tricking you, and they can be awful, mean and horrible sometimes. So always be careful about the friends that you make. Friendship can be very difficult. This reminds me of a line from Little Pony – Princess Twilight said: 'friendship isn't always easy, but there is no doubt it's worth fighting for'. That is definitely true. (Rose, 8)

Introduction

Over the course of this book, we have discussed autism and how autism is generally perceived, from a number of different angles. And in simple terms, it has become apparent that while autistic children might need help and support in school as a result of specific autistic traits, other factors – such as the environment, or the attitude of adults – are just as impactful, if not more so. Therefore, given that school presents arguably the greatest test of social skill for children from a very young age, let us now turn to the question of socialisation, to consider whether similar issues apply.

I spent a lot of my older teens and 20s being told 'you'll like it when you get there' about group socialising. This was never true, but I kept trying. It was obvious to me that I was missing something – the non-autistic people really did seem to enjoy it. I didn't feel that I was missing out on anything; when I say 'missing something' I mean that I just didn't 'get it'. With strangers, one-to-one can be terrifying; there's so much pressure to engage in conversation and to 'perform';

> I feel like I'm under a huge magnifying glass that exposes all. It's painful, I want to run away. (Kabie)

In this chapter, I describe the social complexities that autistic children face in school and discuss why some parents prioritise socialisation as an educational priority more than any other. I also consider social skills training and explain how autistic children might be missing out on the more natural social opportunities that schools usually offer. There is, additionally, the question of bullying, undoubtedly a serious issue for some autistic children, as well as the fact that schools might erroneously apply a model of socialisation – one based on non-autistic children – which doesn't actually work. I also describe how my study revealed that different approaches to the socialisation of autistic children in school – especially when their interests are encouraged – could help create more positive circumstances and outcomes in this area.

Social difficulties

Difficulties in social interaction are deemed to be a core feature of autism (WHO 2018; Wing and Gould 1979). As we saw in Chapter 1, the DSM-5 (APA 2013) refers to 'persistent deficits in social communication and social interaction across multiple contexts', as well as 'deficits in social-emotional reciprocity' and an 'abnormal social approach' as being part of the diagnostic criteria for autism.[1] According to Batten et al. (2006, p.5), such characteristics can be especially problematic in schools, arguing that 'difficulty with social relationships, ranging from being withdrawn, to appearing aloof and indifferent, to simply not fitting in' and seeming 'insensitive to the feelings of others' can all lead to social rejection and bullying. Similarly, Dean et al. (2013, p.148) argue that an autistic girl is shunned by her peers 'because of rigidity, a tendency to fixate on details, repetitive behaviours, and difficulties with problem solving'. In addition, it has been argued that when teachers experience 'challenging behaviour' from autistic pupils, this leads to poor staff–pupil relationships and in turn, rejection of the autistic children by peers (Humphrey and Symes

---

1   See www.cdc.gov/ncbddd/autism/hcp-dsm.html

2011). According to some accounts, therefore, it is the very nature of autism itself that leads to social difficulties and even bullying.

Research also shows that loneliness and isolation can be a major problem for autistic children and young people (Bauminger and Kasari 2003; Humphrey and Symes 2011), which perhaps explains why parents tend to emphasise social outcomes as being the most important priority in school (Dockrell *et al.* 2012). I found the same in my own study, with some of the parents making it clear that their children's friendships were of paramount importance, unlike the school staff, who did not place a strong emphasis on socialisation as an educational priority for the autistic children. Some parents stressed the role of continuity of relationships with peers from pre-school, into primary school and later into secondary school as being key components of happiness and educational inclusion for their autistic children. In fact, two of the ten parents identified developing social skills as the *only* educational priority for their children in primary school.

■ Socialising with more than one person at once isn't something that I naturally like or that I'm drawn to; some people seem to like to go out as a group of friends specifically to be in a group, but that's not something that I really understand the attraction of. In a group it's difficult to have a conversation, it takes huge effort to try to filter out others talking – it's exhausting. (Kabie)

■ Making friends at school I think is important but not the most important thing at school. I like making friends, because you learn about other people, and maybe get help from them sometimes. (Rose, 8)

Moreover, having visited the local special school, the parents in my study felt that the children there lacked social skills, and thought that mainstream schools could offer their child positive role models that special schools could not. And despite this unfortunate manifestation of 'othering', the parents also feared their children would face social rejection and bullying in secondary school, meaning they would consider placing their children in a special school at this point. Indeed, data from the DfE (2016b) suggests that a number of autistic children do not transfer from mainstream primary school to mainstream secondary school, indicating that, in this respect, the parents' anxieties were justified.

- I don't mind getting up in front of people and talking. I find one-to-one stressful. I treat all social engagements with caution. I dislike crowded, rowdy rooms. (Jon)

- I'm very happy with the friends I've got. I like making friends but it's a bit hard to remember their names. But once you get used to seeing them, you can start to remember what they look like and their names. (Rose, 8)

Furthermore, while most of the autistic adults in my study did not mention socialisation when asked specifically about educational priorities, they made a number of comments in other parts of our interviews, which suggested that they had found school socially complex and stressful (Locke *et al.* 2010). Some had wanted to join in with games at play time, but didn't know how to, or were painfully aware of being socially excluded by their peers. Unstructured times, such as breaks and lunchtimes, were the periods when social situations were considered to be at their most difficult (Sainsbury 2009). Social rules and protocol were confusing, especially once they progressed from infants to junior school, when their peers were found to be less accepting. Some of the autistic adults also felt there was a disconnect between themselves and the other children socially; friendships had been difficult to form, or their energies were consumed by simply trying to cope with the noise (Wood 2018a).

- In primary school, when they're little and they don't see differences between everyone...they've already got a built-in non-judgementalism. People get judgemental as they get older. (George)

- The worst time was playgrounds. Running around and screaming – I always found that very difficult. You want to join in, but you can't because it seems alien. (Jon)

- I didn't have any friends but I'm not sure I wanted any. In break times, I mostly stayed inside, either tidying cupboards or doing other odd jobs on my own or in the staffroom making teas and coffees. This suited me well; the playground was too noisy and chaotic and I'd sometimes get into fights. (Kabie)

PE could also be problematic in this respect, as team games and group activities created social or sensory difficulties. Indeed, these issues also impacted on school tests, because, as discussed in Chapter 4, some of the autistic adults said they had feared having attention drawn to them in class if their marks were read out loud, regardless of whether it was a high or low result. Some said that even disappointment at not getting full marks, for example, could be misinterpreted as arrogance, which suggests a need for greater understanding from teachers and peers, as well as help in navigating the social complexities of school (Locke *et al.* 2010). These issues underline the fact that autistic children can experience a number of social difficulties in school, which impact negatively on their well-being (White and Roberson-Nay 2009).

Social skills training

No doubt because of these problems, training in social skills can be considered an important part of the school curriculum of autistic children (Parsons *et al.* 2011), perhaps involving small groups to support their social interaction skills (McConnell 2002). However, the evidence base for this sort of intervention is mixed. Mesibov (1984), for example, found improvements in the social skills of 15 autistic adolescents following a training programme, and Laugeson *et al.* (2012) had similar findings from a parent-mediated intervention. On the other hand, a review of the literature by Rao, Beidel and Murray (2008) concluded that the empirical evidence for these types of intervention was 'minimal'. In addition, Bottema-Beutal *et al.* (2018) argue that the content of social skills' curricula might serve to reduce authentic interactions and increase the stigmatisation of autistic pupils.

In my own study, the potential for stigmatisation was certainly evident, as children were taken out of lessons for some sort of intervention, and so were segregated from their peers and the more natural interactions time in the classroom might permit. In these circumstances, their social choices seemed to evaporate, as the autistic children were placed in a 'special needs' group, and perhaps expected to 'socialise', regardless of any personal preferences on their part. Indeed, sometimes the children were taken off the school premises altogether for therapeutic input, an arrangement that made them more, not less, socially conspicuous. This doesn't mean that time spent away from peers is always *wrong*, as such, but rather highlights the inherent contradiction in this circumstance.

Furthermore, as discussed in Chapter 7, children who spent a lot of time with TAs also experienced unnecessary segregation and stigma, especially those who were 'velcroed' to them (Liasidou 2012), as this marked out the children as being different from their peers (Humphrey and Lewis 2008). Therefore, the presence of support staff, if not effectively planned, can prevent integration with the rest of the class (Sharples *et al.* 2015), while social interactions amongst autistic children have been found to be better if there is less adult involvement (Guldberg 2010).

I like playing football with my friends. (Zack, 10)

In addition, if autistic children are sometimes denied access to the more evident social opportunities with peers in the classroom, they are also unable to benefit from the social environments after-school clubs might provide (Wood 2018b). For example, as discussed in Chapter 3, most of the autistic children in my cohort were unable to attend a regular club out of usual school hours, with school staff citing lack of funding as the reason why they couldn't participate.

The most fun thing I have ever done in school is a trip to a gallery. (James, 8)

In these ways you can see that there is a further contradiction between supposedly supporting the social skills of autistic children, while creating barriers to their social integration at the same time. And so, even if autistic children can benefit from support for socialisation in schools, sometimes the very measures school staff are taking to address the purported social difficulties of the autistic children simply sow the seeds for their further alienation from their peers. At the same time, preventing access to more natural social opportunities is highly problematic too.

Bullying

If feeling socially included is a desirable aim in school, then bullying and social exclusion represent the opposite of this. According to Batten *et al.* (2006), over 40 per cent of autistic children have been bullied at school, which not only puts their emotional well-being at risk, but also disrupts their education:

> Where children have been bullied, 62% of their parents say that the bullying led to them having to miss or change schools or to their child refusing to go to school at all. (Batten *et al.* 2006, p.16)

Similarly, according to Humphrey and Symes (2011, p.42), autistic children are up to three times more likely to be bullied than other children, and they consider 'the social outcomes' of autistic pupils in mainstream schools to be potentially 'very negative'. Hebron and Humphrey (2013) also found that autistic children are more likely to be bullied than children without SEND or those who have other types of special educational need, while for Humphrey and Lewis (2008, p.24), 'social isolation, loneliness and bullying' are 'commonplace' for autistic children. Whitaker (2007) also noted a high level of concern amongst parents that their children were being bullied. And as we have already seen, teachers can play a crucial role in facilitating the social approval of autistic children, because if teachers have a difficult relationship with them, peers are less likely to accept them socially (Robertson, Chamberlain and Kasari 2003).

Some of the autistic adults in my study had experienced bullying in school, being particularly at risk during breaks and lunchtimes. Unfortunately, as discussed in Chapter 7, these are the times of day when autistic children could be receiving little or even no support at all.

> I soon got to equate a break time with other people's cruelty. At school you're fighting a completely alien landscape and the things you are attached to are ripped from you. This doesn't mean that there's not an attachment to people as well. When people mistreat you, you learn not to trust them. (Jon)

For Norwich and Kelly (2004), the responsibility for this situation might rest with the process of mainstream inclusion itself, while according to Cigman (2007), the bullying of autistic children is almost inevitable in mainstream schools. However, for Milton and Sims (2016), it is societal 'othering' and the act of marking out autistic people as 'different' that can lead to bullying rather than the intrinsic nature of autism itself.

> If we can instil at an early age that everyone is different, everyone is okay, we can maybe make some progress. (George)

The role of interests

We have already seen in previous chapters how enabling autistic children to access their interests can bring a range of benefits in terms of their communication, education and general well-being (Winter-Messiers 2007). Perhaps unsurprisingly, therefore, and although there were some exceptions to this, it was evident in my study that when the intense interests of autistic children were supported, this often helped their socialisation too (Gunn and Delafield-Butt 2016; Wood 2019). For example, one boy really liked action heroes, and on an occasion when he was reading a newspaper article on the same subject, another child started looking for similar articles. Another boy who loved Maths invented games based on number patterns, which he would enact with his friends during break times. Moreover, when the autistic children were given the opportunity to engage with their interests, they often required much less support from the TA, meaning it was much easier for other children to approach them and engage with them (Wood 2019). Therefore, the problem of the 'velcro model' of TA support, which can significantly hinder the socialisation of autistic children in schools (Millar *et al.* 2002), is reduced.

Some of the autistic adults in my study had overcome social difficulties experienced in early school years when they developed shared interests with other children, and indeed, these interests had also impacted significantly on their higher education and career choices (Grove *et al.* 2018). This point underscores the fact that if parents fear loneliness and isolation for their children in the future, these problems are less likely to arise if the children are enabled through their education to follow their deeply held interests (Koenig and Williams 2017; Wood 2019).

I do get on with a lot of the people in my class because we all have similar interests. What I find difficult is lots of people I don't know, very massive things like conventions about things I don't have an interest in, e.g. a Dogs Trust convention with the family – there were far too many people. But when I went to a LEGO® convention, I didn't find the number of people difficult whatsoever. (George)

Some things are better in a group, though, and so there's a point; bowling, for example, I could play on my own or with one other person. But a small group is more fun. (Kabie)

I like playing on my Xbox with my friend – it's fun. (Zack, 10)

In addition, some of the school staff spoke very warmly about the rapport they had with the children they supported, and considered that the presence of autistic children greatly benefited their classmates socially. For example, one teacher said that because an autistic boy in his class was good-natured and friendly, this taught his peers kindness and understanding. Another teacher even found that because she and an autistic boy shared the same interests, this created a myriad of opportunities for her to understand how to include him in the curriculum and assessment, as well as creating a bond she felt she didn't share with any other child (Wood 2019).

Therefore, while some school staff and parents in my study expressed concerns that the intense interests of the autistic children created barriers to their socialisation (because they would insist on talking about or playing with what interested them, regardless of what their peers wanted to do), overall there were a number of social advantages to supporting their interests. Indeed, in some cases, the dynamic changed entirely: the autistic child was no longer the child with 'needs', but facilitated the pedagogy and self-knowledge of the teacher and created opportunities for the social learning of the other children too.

Social differences

According to Dean *et al.* (2013, p.148), 'in order to be accepted', an autistic pupil must be prepared to change and adapt because 'the student with ASD is held responsible for upholding the same cultural norms as typical populations'. However, the social benefits that can ensue from enabling autistic children to access their deep interests suggests that rather than coercing them to conform to a way of engaging with others that is contrary to their nature, it is precisely the opposite process which is more likely to prove fruitful.

> Being social has to be my choice. My mum used to push me into a room with other children and expect me to get on. Equally, all autistic people aren't going to automatically get on either. But I think autistic people need challenging – you need to challenge yourself to put yourself in situations which you might find uncomfortable. (Jon)

For Milton (2014b, p.1), for example, there is a 'qualitative difference' to autistic sociality that has been both misunderstood and misrepresented as a flaw. Indeed, Heasman and Gillespie (2018) found that autistic people have distinct ways of communicating and interacting socially with each other that are highly effective. Furthermore, Grinker (2015, p.345) asserts that if we fail to perceive 'the positive characteristics of autism', we might also prevent 'the new forms of sociality' and the 'new social identities' that the societal inclusion of autistic people might permit. Therefore, by simply pathologising the ways in which autistic children prefer to socialise, we miss important opportunities to learn from them that could also benefit their peers.

> The only places where I actively enjoy groups is in autistic space: this is because people generally are more able to be respectful and not talk over each other. I find that autistic spaces have different social dynamics that make it much easier to socialise in a relaxed way. For me autism has been a label that has enabled me to connect with other autistic people, to meet friends and join a community that I couldn't have found without that label. It has enabled me to create a positive identity and to belong. Before I knew I was autistic I didn't belong anywhere, I didn't have a positive identity, I felt alone in a world where others were different. (Kabie)

> At school I had a single best friend, which was all I could cope with. I used to be quite solitary before I had my one best friend – I would be looking at the birds or the dust. There's a difference between being alone and being lonely. (Jon)

Furthermore, it is very important not to generalise when considering the social inclusion of autistic children. Indeed, not all of the autistic adults said they had experienced social difficulties in school or were concerned about friendship-making. Similarly, even though some of the autistic children in my study emphasised friendships as being an important aspect of their time in school, and valued the social aspects of learning, others did not, and preferred to work alone. So this underscores the fact that a nuanced and individualised approach is required when considering the social needs of autistic children in the school environment. Indeed, Wittemeyer *et al.* (2011b, p.19) asserted that 'a striking outcome' of their study was the wish that 'neurotypicals' would stop imposing on autistic people their own views of what they wanted educationally, socially and in the longer term.

> I prefer socialising online when there's actually not a face there. But in situations where I do have to communicate with other people

face to face, I like to take it slow, I like to get to know people. But when I know people, I like to be with a large group. It doesn't matter numbers-side as long as I know them all. I quite regularly find at college that I am talking to 20 people at a time. (George)

I find that autistic people, mostly girls, tend to have one particular best friend that they do everything with, and take with them everywhere. I think that it's important for the teachers to understand that for an autistic girl, you simply can't split her up from her best friend. For me, I used to cry when I was in a separate group than my best friend for something because she was the best thing in my entire life at that point and she meant everything to me, so being separated, even for one lesson, was devastating to me. I always had other friends in school, but none was equally important to me, or just as awesome, as my best friend was. This was a huge deal for me in primary school…but even in secondary school I still go everywhere and do everything with my best friend, so I think it's important for secondary and primary school teachers to understand this and the impact it can have if an autistic girl is separated from her BFF (best friends forever). (Grace, 14)

It's almost a pure friendship with objects – with people it gets very muddled. An attachment to an object is so much easier. No wonder you end up acting strangely when people are confusing and they want to take away your friends. (Jon)

I didn't really have any friends at primary school; it wasn't that I wanted friends or didn't want friends, I was kind of neutral about it, I didn't find the other kids particularly interesting. I enjoyed learning and that was what school was for. I've always been much better at learning on my own rather than in a group. (Kabie)

I prefer smaller groups or individuals. (Michael)

Conclusion

Schools are socially complex environments and autistic children, considered to have social difficulties by dint of being autistic, may struggle within them, especially if they are expected to conform to collective norms that are contrary to their nature (Milton 2014b). Moreover, even if some autistic children need help to form friendships and to understand the social intricacies of school, they might be denied the more natural social opportunities that schools usually offer, including out-of-hours clubs and trips. Furthermore, removing a child from class in order to provide some sort of social skills intervention runs the risk not only of stigmatising the child, but also of embedding further the problem of over-zealous TA support, thus separating the child even further from peers.

In addition, autistic children are at particular risk of bullying, especially as they get older, meaning that they should not be left exposed and unsupported at break and lunchtimes, when bullies can dominate. This also underlines the importance of teaching other children about autism, so that they can understand their autistic classmates better. A key element of this is for school staff to form effective relationships with the autistic children themselves, in order to create positive role models of acceptance and engagement for all of their pupils.

More positively, however, enabling autistic children to access their intense interests offers opportunities for greater understanding and friendship-making, although this is not always the case, and it should not be assumed that all autistic children want to make friends with their peers. Indeed, understanding the social dispositions of individual children, and supporting the ways they want to engage and communicate, are much more likely to be beneficial. Overall, it is the quality of relationships – both with school staff and peers – which can be the lynchpin to the effective educational inclusion of autistic children (Jones *et al.* 2008).

Key points

- Any social difficulties experienced by autistic children must be appraised on an individual basis and take into account their social preferences.

- If interventions are implemented to support socialisation, staff must ensure that these approaches do not stigmatise the children.

- Autistic children should be fully supported in the typical social opportunities of school, including clubs and trips, if that is what they want.

- Autistic children can be at a particular risk of bullying, especially in breaks and lunchtimes.

- Enabling autistic children to access their interests could facilitate their socialisation, especially with like-minded peers.

- Autistic children might prefer to socialise in different ways to non-autistic children, who could also learn from them.

Chapter 10

The Future

Introduction

What does the future hold for autistic children and young people? Certainly, if you look at the statistics on health, employment and happiness outcomes, they make for pretty depressing reading (Howlin *et al.* 2013; Wittemeyer *et al.* 2011b). A large-scale study based in Sweden found that autistic people are likely to die on average 16 years earlier than the general population, with those described as 'low functioning' dying – alarmingly – on average under the age of 40 (Hirvikoski *et al.* 2016). Moreover, it was found that this phenomenon is due to a range of health issues, which suggests that it's not because of autism per se (although autism can be accompanied by a number of co-occurring conditions), but because the health needs of autistic people are not being met. The rates for suicide, loneliness and depression are also very concerning (Cassidy *et al.* 2014; Segers and Rawana 2014), and according to a survey run by the National Autistic Society in 2016, only 16 per cent of autistic people are in full-time employment.[1]

Furthermore, despite the weighty legal provisions that support the principles of educational inclusion discussed at different points in this book, it is not at all clear that they are being instigated and acted on. For example, the UN Committee on the Rights of Persons with Disabilities, which monitors the implementation of the CRPD (UN DESA 2006) by nation-states, found that the UK needs to address the issue of the rising numbers of children in special schools or who are experiencing other forms of segregated education (UN Committee on the Rights of Persons with

---

1   https://www.autism.org.uk/get-involved/media-centre/news/2016-10-27-employment-gap.aspx

Disabilities 2017). This suggests that the principle of mainstream educational inclusion still has a long way to go, or indeed might even be going in reverse.

But it's not all bad news, by any means, and so it is also important to look positively towards the future and to acknowledge that there are faint signs of optimism twinkling on the horizon. Nowadays, autistic people are much more likely to be involved in and lead research, and so their vital skills, views and perspectives are beginning to shape priorities and funding initiatives (Fletcher-Watson *et al.* 2018). Some employers, having recognised the potential talents and abilities of autistic people, are actively recruiting autistic people into their organisations. And I hope that by reading this book, whether you are a parent, a teacher, a student or a researcher, autistic or non-autistic, you will have a better understanding of how autistic children can be supported in schools. Because what we all want and need is for autistic children not just to cope or survive within the school environment, but also to flourish and develop their own, individual paths for the future. This will not only help them, but the rest of us too.

■ I feel that it's got to get brighter soon. I feel that society is becoming more and more accepting and it can't be too long before there's going to be a wake-up call allowing progress to be made. (George)

Future education

According to Hesmondhalgh (2006, p.46), if staff 'remain open to the pupils' and are 'willing to learn from them, spend time listening rather than talking', are prepared to 'facilitate their ideas, and aim for their dreams', then 'even the most apparently hostile environment like a secondary school can become autism friendly'. Nevertheless, it's important to underline that full-time education in a mainstream school, even the most accommodating, 'autism-friendly' school on earth, will not necessarily suit all autistic children. There is an urgent need for much more flexible approaches to education, with perhaps part-time home and school placements, for example. According to Slee and Allan (2001, p.186), 'regular schooling was never meant for all comers', and they suggest that genuine inclusive schooling 'may well imply an array of offerings' where 'authenticity of choice and destination' are available. According to Allan (2008, p.9), inclusion as it was originally conceived was about 'increasing participation and removing barriers' rather the issue of educational placement only, because 'schools were never meant to be for everyone' (2008, p.10). Meanwhile, Thomas (2012, p.480) proposes training school staff 'to work across home-school boundaries' in order to facilitate inclusion.

Nevertheless, these perspectives should be accompanied with a note of caution: flexible schooling is not the same as 'off-rolling' pupils ahead of public exams, forcing part-time attendance on a child who is considered difficult to manage (Office of the Children's Commissioner 2012, 2017), or failing to deal constructively with school refusal (Preece and Howley 2018).

Slee and Allan (2001, p.177) also argue that inclusive education should represent 'a fundamental paradigm shift' towards an understanding whereby inclusion is conceived of as a matter for all, not just for certain categories of children. Indeed, in a fascinating case study based in a school in Finland, Tarr, Tsokova and Takkunen (2012) found that terms such as 'inclusion' and 'special education' have very different meanings to how they are commonly used elsewhere. Not only are all children deemed to be in receipt of 'special education' at some point or another during their schooling, but the authors assert that the term 'inclusion' is not used, and 'rarely appears in the lexicon of policy documents or published work' (Tarr *et al.* 2012, p.694). This, they suggest, is because 'inclusion' is a given, rather than an ideal to be debated. From their study, which contained a consideration of the physical layout of the school and how teaching roles were assigned, the authors conclude that the school is an example of how to 'reduce exclusion and isolation through skilful manipulation of the physical, institutional and communicative context' from which they state others 'could draw some valuable lessons' (Tarr *et al.* 2012, p.702).

> I want support for people who wish to and are able to home school – more crossover of different educational systems: why is it that we allow private education to be subsidised but don't give free resources to people who want to home school? In paid-for 'private' education there are better facilities, smaller classes – why can't the general population have that?
>
> I believe that education of children is a whole society responsibility – there are many forms that it could take and we shouldn't get stuck on what's right for all, as all can't be educated in the same way. (Kabie)

What also seems self-evident is that when the needs of autistic children are addressed in the early years of schooling, they are much more likely to have positive longer-term outcomes. This also means that even if autistic children are deemed to have poor functional skills, they should be provided with a motivating learning environment (Jacques *et al.* 2018) and a curriculum likely to provide them with qualifications that they can actually use in the future (DfE 2015a). Moreover, some of the autistic participants in my own study were keen to highlight that for them, being autistic means having certain desirable attributes such as attention to detail, perfectionism, or being able to ignore social distractions and focus instead on the task in hand. Therefore, it is vital that educators understand and value these traits in autistic children, should they possess them, while providing additional support for their learning if required.

I'm currently studying a Level 3 qualification on computers. I've not got a set job in mind – computing will be used a lot in the foreseeable future, so having a very good knowledge of it is going to look great on my CV. (George)

There seems to be an attitude that if a child doesn't learn then the problem is theirs. This is applied to all kids, not just autistic or other disabled kids. (Kabie)

A teacher needs to know that with an autistic child – they need to take a leap of faith and assume that nothing that works for them will work for that child, because they see the world totally differently. (Jon)

My interests have had little bearing on my career but my positive autistic traits, such as my focus, attention to detail, technical ability and problem-solving skills, are what has got me into the role I currently have and are key to performing well at my job. The vast amount of data analysis I do within my job requires all of these skills to a great extent. (Michael)

I'm not 100 per cent sure just yet, but I would like to go either down the path of artist/animator or animal conservationist as they are the things I am most passionate about. (Grace, 14)

I want to be an actor like James Cagney. (James, 8)

I want to be an app maker. My hobby is now trying to create ideas for apps. I want to be able to make my apps in real life. Or possibly be a YouTuber, because I really like YouTube. Or customising ponies, like changing their colours. Maybe I can do both – I can create an app to change ponies. (Rose, 8)

I love cooking at school – I've made a pizza and pasta, and I made a chocolate Yule log at Christmas. But I don't think I can be a chef because I'm not good enough. I don't know what I want to do in the future. I'd like to live somewhere quiet by the coast, or in the countryside. I'd like to live on my own – I don't want to get married or have children. (Zack, 10)

It is also clear that the physical school environment, if it is not carefully managed, can be inherently exclusionary for autistic children, with noise arguably the biggest culprit (Wood 2018a). This is why the principles of universal design – which would mean that schools are planned from the outset to accommodate a diversity of learners – are so important (Liasidou 2012). Nevertheless, especially with the pressures on space described in Chapter 2, there are no easy answers, although Woolner and Hall (2010) recommend involving the whole school community in decisions about noise and break times, for example. In addition, McAllister and Sloan (2016) advise that autistic children and young people should be involved in the design of their own learning environments.

There needs to be much more flexibility. Also, a greater understanding that autistic kids may not be motivated about the same things or in the same way as non-autistic kids. Class sizes need to be reduced – they are way too large, too many other kids, too much noise, too much 'visual noise' – pictures on the wall, strung across ceilings, etc. We don't want bland, but some classrooms are so overloading it's painful. I'm a huge fan of universal design – why isn't everyone else? (Kabie)

Furthermore, it's important to recognise that the principle of universal design doesn't just have implications for the physical layout and contents of the school buildings, but also for the curriculum, timetable, and even attitudes. Indeed, the CRPD (UN DESA 2006) refers to 'attitudinal' as well as 'environmental' barriers that can hinder the 'full and effective participation in society' of disabled people (UN DESA 2006, preamble (e)). In addition, it certainly seems the case that if the strong interests of autistic children are incorporated flexibly into different aspects of school life, this could potentially provide a range of inclusionary benefits.

You work to the child's skillset and interests. There are bits that we won't want to do and there are bits we'll be able to do marvellously. Maybe you target the child's special interests and widen it for them. (Jon)

■ I really like learning how to do Manga-style drawings. It also teaches me how to do other things better, not just Manga-style drawings. (Rose, 8)

The CRPD (UN DESA 2006) asserts the importance of 'main-streaming disability issues' (preamble (g)), and that disabled children have the right to be taught by well-trained staff, including teachers with disabilities, as there must be 'respect for the right of children to preserve their identities' (Article 3). So, we must ask a further question: how many school head teachers, SENCOs, teachers and learning support assistants are autistic? And let's say, if 1 in 100 school staff were known to be autistic (taking our most conservative population prevalence measure from Chapter 1), how much would this knowledge benefit autistic pupils in a school? Just think of the advantages to other school staff if their autistic colleagues could help inform the ways in which autistic children are supported. And how valuable it would be for all pupils, but especially those who are autistic, to have autistic role models in their school, such as their teachers or senior staff. And if it is the case that very few school staff are autistic, why is this? Are there barriers that prevent autistic people from becoming educators? Do autistic school staff fear prejudice if they are open about their diagnosis? This is certainly an area I hope to research in the future.

■ I think that well-trained autistic teachers and support staff plus conversations about being autistic, autistic culture, etc. should be a norm; sometimes teachers (and parents) don't even want to mention the word 'autism' as they feel it would have a detrimental impact on the autistic kids, but everyone should be encouraged to explore who they are and create a positive self-image. (Kabie)

Future research
Throughout this book, while highlighting the examples of good practice I observed, I have been critical of some of the attitudes and approaches of the school staff in my study. However, I have also made it clear that those same staff could be working under

difficult circumstances, being expected to support a diversity of learners with insufficient resources. Indeed, the question is not so much whether educators are good at their jobs, but rather what the conditions are which enable them to do their work well.

As discussed in Chapter 7, one finding from my research was that even when school staff showed a high degree of empathy and understanding towards the autistic children, they still considered they didn't really know anything about autism and feared that they weren't 'experts'. They felt that 'expertise' lay elsewhere, usually in the form of visiting professionals, such as speech and language therapists. While these staff might not have been 'experts' in autism (because frankly, no one really is: even autistic people are not necessarily 'experts' in autism), it is concerning that they would set aside their own perceptions and knowledge acquired through spending time with an autistic child, and place faith in a vague professional who might not have met that child. Some of the parents had a similar attitude, despite having known their own child since birth. And so, in my view, there is an urgent need, not only to create more circumstances whereby school staff at all levels can inform and conduct research, but for research to be enlightened by caregivers too.

In addition, in Chapter 1, I touched briefly on issues of gender, an area of increasing focus in autism research. Over recent years there has been a significant rise in attention paid to the ways in which autism might be manifested in women and girls (Carpenter, Happé and Egerton 2019), and research suggests that autistic girls in schools can be especially at risk of having their needs overlooked (Moyse and Porter 2014; Sproston, Sedgewick and Crane 2017), so they either experience exclusion or withdraw entirely from school. Indeed, this arguably points to a wider problem whereby autistic children who are not creating problems for others are much less likely to receive the right support. Even so, Stewart (2016) is of the view that because more women and girls are now being diagnosed with autism, there has been a shift in the narrative of autism and poor outcomes, given that some of these women at least are 'successful', although it is not clear whether this is because of, despite – or even simply coincidental to – being autistic.

■ Other girls my age are all obsessed with wearing make-up (which should be completely banned in school), having designer handbags (instead of backpacks which are much more practical for school), posting 'sexy' selfies and pictures on social media and having all the latest trendy clothing. It drives me mad that girls waste time with all this when they really should be focusing on school and getting good grades, but a lot of them just don't care. (Grace, 14)

There are also fierce debates as to whether there are, in fact, distinct autism traits delineated by gender, and if it is even helpful to think about autism along such binary constructs (Kourti and MacLeod 2018). Meanwhile, ideas about gender fluidity and diversity and non-binary identities are also acquiring greater importance, especially as there is evidence that autistic people are more likely to identify in a non-binary way (Walsh *et al.* 2018). There is also the issue of gender dysphoria – when there is a misalignment between a person's biological sex and gender identity – which is considered to be more prevalent amongst autistic people (Glidden *et al.* 2016; Lawson 2015). Therefore, while learning about relationships and sex should be prioritised for autistic children and young people as much as for anyone else, sex education in schools also needs to take into account the specific needs of autistic people (Hannah and Stagg 2016), and incorporate questions of gender identity and sensory issues, for example (Barnett and Maticka-Tyndale 2015).

There are further complexities in the autism research context due to the fact that when the views of autistic adults are sought, more women than men tend to come forward (Kapp *et al.* 2013; Kenny *et al.* 2016). Significant gender imbalances were evident in my own study: amongst the children there were nine autistic boys, but only one girl. However, I had eight female adult autistic participants, and only two male. There were other divisions along gender lines: only 5 from the 36 school staff in my study were male, and 9 of the 10 parents were female (although it should be noted that I did not ask any of the participants about gender identity). This phenomenon, along with other questions of representativeness to do with the limited number of minimally verbal autistic people involved in research, shows that there is still some way to go before the full diversity of autistic children and adults are accounted for in studies about autism.

The question must also be asked as to whether research conducted along gender binary lines is sustainable in the longer term.

Other research developments at a relatively early stage concern the use of technology to support communication (Murray and Lawson 2007). As I suggested in Chapter 8, technological devices could be used much more extensively in schools, and it is essential that staff receive the necessary training to be able to assist autistic pupils who might benefit significantly from their use. If support staff are 'low tech', they are unlikely to be able to help autistic children who need technology to be able to communicate and learn. The use of 'wearable tech' is another area of research in its relative infancy: these could provide teachers with important information about the anxiety levels of the autistic children in their class, for example (Sano and Picard 2013).

> I want autistic people with a learning disability and/or who do not communicate verbally or are minimally verbal to be welcomed and included and accepted. The autistic community is trying with this, but we could do better. Too many times I hear non-autistic (and some autistic) people talking of 'high functioning', using IQ as a trophy, doing what they can to separate out people who are autistic but 'not like me'. In some cases, this is from people who have never met the people they are stigmatising in this way, that they are degrading. I want autistic people and others to recognise their privilege and to use that to improve things for all. (Kabie)

In 2013, Pellicano *et al.* found that in the context of the UK, more than half of the autism research published and funded was 'devoted to understanding more about the underlying biology, brain and cognition of autistic people' (2013, pp.4–5). This compared starkly with areas such as complementary therapies and sensory-based treatments, for example, where in 2011, there were no publications at all within the search criteria (Pellicano *et al.* 2013, p.27). Furthermore, for their participants who were drawn from the broader autism community, biological research was not a priority, but rather they felt the focus of autism research 'should lie in the areas of public services, promoting the life chances of autistic people and how autistic people think and learn' (2013, p.35). Given the poor employment, education and health outcomes of autistic people, this suggests a need to focus much more on the areas that would make a real difference to their daily lives. This includes the area of epilepsy, which autistic people are more likely to develop than the rest of the population, sometimes with fatal consequences (Woolfenden *et al.* 2012).

■ Overall, I personally hope there are improvements at a soon point. We're living in a society that is bringing up every other group and improving their lives. We've got to be on that list somewhere and soon. We = people with disabilities, especially those that aren't visible disabilities. At the moment, you wouldn't dare do anything so mean as to force a person in a wheelchair to climb up stairs, but you've got the equivalent with us, and because it can't be seen so they get away with it. There's an expectation that people with autism will just set aside their difficulties, which they would never do with someone with a physical difficulty. (George)

■ I want autistic people to be viewed as equal. I want people to stop talking of cure and burden. I'd like to see more flexibility in all services so that 'reasonable adjustments' aren't such a big deal and we just care more about how to accommodate everyone. I want to see within my lifetime that autistic people no longer suffer from health inequality, no longer die younger than the non-disabled population; that co-occurring conditions such as epilepsy are understood and that deaths from epilepsy or suicide become rare – currently these are two big killers of autistic people. (Kabie)

■ Better understanding. Acceptance. The voice of actually autistic people is listened to – old or young. Less stereotypes in the media, because that influences the way autistic people are looked at and treated. More understanding of mental health and autism. Better sense of belonging. I would love the next generations not to have to go through what we have, because of greater awareness and understanding. Actually autistic people should be leading this work, not 'specialists' who do not have lived experience of being autistic. If you want to know what the experience of visiting the pyramids is like, you would ask someone who has actually been to the pyramids and experienced it, not someone who'd seen a picture in a book or on a map. If you want to ask what an autistic person needs, then

just ask that autistic person what they need, not assume or read a
book about it. (Jon)

■ I hope for autistic people's potentials to be recognised, both in the
classroom and in employment, and for people to be more positive
about what autistic people can offer to society. There is too much
stigma and not enough readily available support out there. (Michael)

It is also important to be cognisant of the fact that autistic children
do not remain forever in infancy, but grow older and become
autistic adults. Yet there is a dearth of research into the needs of
older autistic adults (Happé and Charlton 2012; Michael 2016), with
the majority of studies devoted to children (Pellicano *et al.* 2013).

Fortunately, autistic-led groups such as the Autism Rights Group
Highland (ARGH) (co-founded by Kabie Brook), the Participatory
Autism Research Collective in the UK and in the USA, the Autistic
Self-Advocacy Network and others, show that autistic people are
gradually starting to dominate the narrative about the priorities
for research, as well as helping to reshape attitudes towards autism
and promote more accepting concepts such as neurodiversity.
According to Thibault (2014, p.80), for example, autistic people are
themselves 'redefining autism' and in so doing, they are 'creating
new spaces in the cultural landscape, shifting boundaries,
changing old paradigms and altering abnormality discourses'.
Ultimately, it is only by facilitating, accepting and acting on the
views and perspectives of a diversity of autistic children and
adults that we can begin to address the problems experienced by
autistic children in schools. I hope that by reading a book that is
substantially informed by the opinions and experiences of autistic
people – 20 in my original study, combined with 10 for this book,
with many autistic authors cited within it – you will have a better
understanding of how to enable autistic children to learn, excel and
flourish in school, and so have better futures.

References

AAA (Ambitious About Autism) (2012) *Schools Report 2012*. London: AAA.

AAA (2013) *Schools Report 2013*. London: AAA.

AAA (2016) *When Will ~~They~~ We Learn?* London: AAA.

Acheson, K. (2008) 'Silence as gesture: Rethinking the nature of communicative silences.' *Communication Theory 18*, 4, 535–555.

Alexander, R. (2000) *Culture and Pedagogy: International Comparisons in Primary Education*. Oxford and Cambridge, MA: Blackwell Publishers Ltd.

Allan, J. (2008) *Rethinking Inclusive Education: The Philosophers of Difference in Practice*. Dordrecht: Springer.

Allan, J. (2010) 'The sociology of disability and the struggle for inclusive education.' *British Journal of Sociology of Education 31*, 5, 603–619.

Allan, J. and Youdell, D. (2017) 'Ghostings, materialisations and flows in Britain's special educational needs and disability assemblage.' *Discourse: Studies in the Cultural Politics of Education 38*, 1, 70–82.

Amanda Baggs Controversy (2009) 'Presentation and discussion of the Amanda Baggs Controversy.' Available at http://abaggs.blogspot.co.uk/#One, accessed on 3 January 2017.

APA (American Psychiatric Association) (2013) *Diagnostic and Statistical Manual of Mental Disorders, 5th Edition (DSM-5)*. Washington, DC: APA.

Armstrong, D., Galloway, D. and Tomlinson, S. (1993) 'Assessing special educational needs: The child's contribution.' *British Educational Research Journal 19*, 2, 121–131.

Arnold, L. (2010) 'Genetics, eugenics and autism. It is not too late for action.' Luscus: The Blog of the One-Eyed King, 3 January. Available at https://laurentius-rex.blogspot.co.uk/2010/01/genetics-eugenics-and-autism-it-is-not.html, accessed on 9 September 2017.

Arnold, L. (2013) 'The social construction of the savant.' *Autonomy, the Critical Journal of Interdisciplinary Autism Studies 1*, 2, 1–8.

Ashburner, J., Ziviani, J. and Rodger, S. (2008) 'Sensory processing and classroom emotional, behavioral, and educational outcomes in children with autism spectrum disorder.' *The American Journal of Occupational Therapy 62*, 564–573.

Baggs, A. (2006) 'In My Language' [video]. Available at www.youtube.com/watch?v=JnylM1hl2jc, accessed on 12 December 2014.

Baio, J., Wiggins, L., Christensen, D., Maenner, M. *et al.* (2018) 'Prevalence of autism spectrum disorder among children aged 8 years – Autism and Developmental Disabilities Monitoring Network, 11 sites, United States, 2014.' *Morbidity and Mortality Weekly Report Surveillance Summary 67*, SS-6, 1–23.

Baird, G., Simonoff, E., Pickles, A., Chandler, S. *et al.* (2006) 'Prevalence of disorders of the autism spectrum in a population cohort of children in South Thames: The Special Needs and Autism Project (SNAP).' *The Lancet 368*, 9531, 210–215.

Barnett, J.P. and Maticka-Tyndale, E. (2015) 'Qualitative exploration of sexual experiences among adults on the autism spectrum: Implications for sex education.' *Perspectives on Sexual and Reproductive Health 47*, 4, 171–179.

Baron-Cohen, S. (2002a) 'Is Asperger Syndrome necessarily viewed as a disability?' *Focus on Autism and Developmental Disabilities 17*, 3, 186–191.

Baron-Cohen, S. (2002b) 'The extreme male brain theory of autism.' *TRENDS in Cognitive Sciences 6*, 6, 248–253.

Baron-Cohen, S. and Wheelwright, S. (1999) '"Obsessions" in children with autism or Asperger syndrome: A content analysis in terms of core domains of cognition.' *British Journal of Psychiatry 175*, 5, 484–490.

Baron-Cohen, S., Leslie, A. and Frith, U. (1985) 'Does the autistic child have a "theory of mind"?' *Cognition 21*, 1, 37–46.

Baron-Cohen, S., Scahill, V., Izaguirre, J. and Hornsey, H. (1999) 'The prevalence of Gilles de la Tourette syndrome in children and adolescents with autism: A large scale study.' *Psychological Medicine 29*, 5, 1151–1159.

Baron-Cohen, S., Wheelwright, S., Burtenshaw, A. and Hobson, E. (2007) 'Mathematical talent is linked to autism.' *Human Nature 18*, 2, 125–131.

Baron-Cohen, S., Ashwin, E., Ashwin, C., Tavassoli, T. and Chakrabarti, B. (2009a) 'Talent in autism: Hyper-systemizing, hyper-attention to detail and sensory hypersensitivity.' *Philosophical Transactions of the Royal Society B 364*, 1377–1383.

Baron-Cohen, S., Scott, F.J., Allison, C., Williams, J. *et al.* (2009b) 'Prevalence of autism-spectrum conditions: UK school-based population study.' *British Journal of Psychiatry 194*, 6, 500–509.

Baron-Cohen, S., Johnson, D., Asher, J., Wheelwright, S. *et al.* (2013) 'Is synaesthesia more common in autism?' *Molecular Autism 4*, 40, 1–6.

Bartak, L., Rutter, M. and Cox, A. (1975) 'A comparative study of infantile autism and specific developmental receptive language disorder: 1. The children.' *The British Journal of Psychiatry 126*, 2, 127–145.

Barthes, R. (1968) 'La mort de l'auteur.' *Manteia*, 61–67.

Barton, M. (2012) *It's Raining Cats and Dogs: An Autism Spectrum Guide to the Confusing World of Idioms, Metaphors and Everyday Expressions.* London: Jessica Kingsley Publishers.

Batten, A., Corbett, C., Rosenblatt, M., Withers, L. and Yuille, R. (2006) *Autism and Education: The Reality for Families Today.* London: NAS Publications.

Bauminger, N. and Kasari, C. (2003) 'Loneliness and friendship in high-functioning children with autism.' *Child Development 71*, 2, 447–456.

BBC Science & Nature (2006) 'The Woman Who Thinks like a Cow.' Available at www.bbc.co.uk/sn/tvradio/programmes/horizon/broadband/tx/temple/, accessed on 17 September 2017.

Bearne, E. (ed.) (1996) *Differentiation and Diversity in the Primary School.* London: Routledge.

Bogdashina, O. (2010) *Autism and the Edges of the Known World: Sensitivities, Language and Constructed Reality.* London: Jessica Kingsley Publishers.

Bogdashina, O. (2016) *Sensory Perceptual Issues in Autism and Asperger Syndrome*, 2nd edn. London: Jessica Kingsley Publishers.

Bor, D., Billington, J. and Baron-Cohen, S. (2007) 'Savant memory for digits in a case of synaesthesia and Asperger syndrome is related to hyperactivity in the lateral prefrontal cortex.' *Neurocase 13*, 5-6, 311–319.

Bottema-Beutel, K., Park, H. and Kim, S.Y. (2018) 'Commentary on social skills training curricula for individuals with ASD: Social interaction, authenticity, and stigma.' *Journal of Autism and Developmental Disorders 48*, 3, 953–964.

Boyd, B., Woodward, C. and Bodfish, J. (2011) 'Modified exposure and response prevention to treat the repetitive behaviors of a child with autism: A case report.' *Case Reports in Psychiatry 2011*, 1–5.

Boyd, B., Odom, S., Humphreys, B. and Sam, A. (2010) 'Infants and toddlers with autism spectrum disorder: Early identification and early intervention.' *Journal of Early Intervention 32*, 2, 75–98.

Boyle, C., Boulet, S., Schieve, L., Cohen, R.A. *et al.* (2011) 'Trends in the prevalence of developmental disabilities in US children, 1997–2008.' *Pediatrics 127*, 6, 1034–1042.

Brady, S. (2011) 'Efficacy of Phonics Teaching for Reading Outcomes.' In S. Brady, D. Braze and C. Fowler (eds) *Explaining Individual Differences in Reading: Theory and Evidence* (pp.69–96). New York: Psychology Press.

Brignell, A., Chenausky, K.V., Song, H., Zhu, J., Suo, C. and Morgan, A.T. (2018) 'Communication interventions for autism spectrum disorder in minimally verbal children.' *Cochrane Database of Systematic Reviews 2018* 11, Art. No. CD012324.

Briskman, J., Frith, U. and Happé, F. (2001) 'Exploring the cognitive phenotype of autism: Weak "central coherence" in parents and siblings of children with autism: II. Real-life skills and preferences.' *The Journal of Child Psychology and Psychiatry and Allied Disciplines 42*, 3, 309–316.

Broderick, A.A. and Ne'eman, A. (2008) 'Autism as metaphor: Narrative and counter-narrative.' *International Journal of Inclusive Education 12*, 5–6, 459–476.

Broer, S.M., Doyle, M.B. and Giangreco, M.F. (2005) 'Perspectives of students with intellectual disabilities about their experiences with paraprofessional support.' *Exceptional children 71*, 415–430.

Brugha, T., McManus, S., Bankart, J., Scott. F. *et al.* (2011) 'Epidemiology of autism spectrum disorders in adults in the community in England.' *Archives of General Psychiatry 68*, 5, 459–466.

Buescher, A., Cidav, Z., Knapp, M. and Mandell, D. (2014) 'Costs of autism spectrum disorders in the United Kingdom and the United States.' *JAMA: Journal of American Medical Association Pediatrics 8*, 721–728.

Caldwell, P. (2008) *Using Intensive Interaction and Sensory Integration: A Handbook for Those Who Support People with Severe Autistic Spectrum Disorder.* London: Jessica Kingsley Publishers.

Campbell, T. (2015) 'Stereotyped at seven? Biases in teacher judgement of pupils' ability and attainment.' *Journal of Social Policy 44*, 3, 517–547.

Carpenter, B., Happé, F. and Egerton, J. (eds) (2019) *Girls and Autism: Educational, Family and Personal Perspectives.* Abingdon: Routledge.

Cassidy, S., Bradley, P., Robinson, J., Allison, C., McHugh, M. and Baron-Cohen, S. (2014) 'Suicidal ideation and suicide plans or attempts in adults with Asperger's syndrome attending a specialist diagnostic clinic: A clinical cohort study.' *The Lancet Psychiatry 1*, 2, 142–147.

Chan, J., Lang, R., Rispoli, M., O'Reilly, M., Sigafoos, J. and Cole, H. (2009) 'Use of peer-mediated interventions in the treatment of autism spectrum disorders: A systematic review.' *Research in Autism Spectrum Disorders 3*, 4, 876–889.

Children and Families Act (2014) Available at www.legislation.gov.uk/ukpga/2014/6/contents/enacted, accessed on 6 August 2014.

Christensen, D.L., Baio, J., Braun, K.V., Bilder, D. *et al.* (2016) 'Prevalence and characteristics of autism spectrum disorder among children aged 8 years.' *Morbidity and Mortality Weekly Report 65*, 3. Atlanta, GA: US Department of Health and Human Services, Centers for Disease Control and Prevention. Available at http://dx.doi.org/10.15585/mmwr.ss6503a1

Cigman, R. (ed.) (2007) *Included or Excluded? The Challenge of Mainstream for Some SEN Children.* Abingdon: Routledge.

Colenbrander, D., Nickels, L. and Kohnen, S. (2017) 'Similar but different: Differences in comprehension diagnosis on the Neale Analysis of Reading Ability and the York Assessment of Reading for Comprehension.' *Journal of Research in Reading 40*, 4, 403–419.

Cook, A., Ogden, J. and Winstone, N. (2017) 'Friendship motivations, challenges and the role of masking for girls with autism in contrasting school settings.' *European Journal of Special Needs Education 33*, 3, 302–315.

Courchesne, V., Girard, D., Jacques, C. and Soulières, I. (2018) 'Assessing intelligence at autism diagnosis: Mission impossible? Testability and cognitive profile of autistic preschoolers.' *Journal of Autism and Developmental Disorders.* Available at https://doi.org/10.1007/s10803-018-3786-4

Cox, M., Herner, J.G., Demczyk, M.J. and Nieberding, J. (2006) 'Provision of testing accommodations for students with disabilities on statewide assessments: Statistical links with participation and discipline rates.' *Remedial and Special Education 27*, 6, 346–354.

Crais, E.R., Watson, L.R. and Baranek, G.T. (2009) 'Use of gesture development in profiling children's prelinguistic communication skills.' *American Journal of Speech-Language Pathology 18*, 1, 95–108.

Crane, L., Goddard, L. and Pring, L. (2009) 'Sensory processing in adults with autism spectrum disorders.' *Autism 13*, 3, 215–228.

Cremin, H., Thomas, G. and Vincett, K. (2005) 'Working with teaching assistants: Three models evaluated.' *Research Papers in Education 20*, 4, 413–432.

Croll, P. (2002) 'Social deprivation, school-level achievement and SEN.' *Educational Research 44*, 1, 43–53.

Crosland, K. and Dunlap, G. (2012) 'Effective strategies for the inclusion of children with autism in general education classrooms.' *Behavior Modification 36*, 3, 251–269.

Curcio, F. (1978) 'Sensorimotor functioning and communication in mute autistic children.' *Journal of Autism and Childhood Schizophrenia 8*, 3, 281–292.

Davis, J., Watson, N. and Cunningham-Burley, S. (2000) 'Learning the Lives of Disabled Children: Developing a Reflexive Approach.' In P. Christensen and A. James (eds) *Research with Children: Perspectives and Practices* (pp.201–224). Abingdon: Routledge.

Dawson, M. (2010) 'Are you high or low functioning? Examples from autism research.' The Autism Crisis: Science and Ethics in an Era of Autism Politics. Available at http://autismcrisis.blogspot.co.uk/2010/, accessed on 10 October 2017.

Dawson, M., Soulières, I., Gernsbacher, M.A. and Mottron, L. (2007) 'The level and nature of autistic intelligence.' *Psychological Science 18*, 8, 657–662.

Dean, M., Fox Adams, G. and Kasari, C. (2013) 'How narrative difficulties build peer rejection: A discourse analysis of a girl with autism and her female peers.' *Discourse Studies 15*, 2, 147–166.

de Beauvoir, S. (1949) *Le Deuxième Sexe 1*. Paris: Gallimard.

Deb, S. and Prasad, K. (1994) 'The prevalence of autistic disorder among children with a learning disability.' *The British Journal of Psychiatry 165*, 3, 395–399.

De Giacomo, A. and Fombonne, E. (1998) 'Parental recognition of developmental abnormalities in autism.' *European Child & Adolescent Psychiatry 7*, 3, 131–136.

DES (Department for Education and Science) (1978) *Special Educational Needs: Report of the Committee of Enquiry into the Education of Handicapped Children and Young People (The Warnock Report)*. London: HMSO.

DfE (Department for Education) (2010) *Schools, Pupils and their Characteristics: January 2010*. London: DfE. Available at www.gov.uk/government/statistics/schools-pupils-and-their-characteristics-january-2010, accessed on 17 September 2017.

DfE (2011) *Teachers' Standards: Guidance for School Leaders, School Staff and Governing Bodies*. London: DfE. Available at www.gov.uk/government/publications/teachers-standards, accessed on 7 September 2018.

DfE (2012) *Research Evidence on Reading for Pleasure*. DFE-57519-2012. London: DfE.

DfE (2013) *Evidence on Physical Education and Sport in Schools*. DFE-00092-2013. London: DfE.

DfE (2014) *Phonics: Choosing a Programme*. London: DfE. Available at www.gov.uk/government/collections/phonics-choosing-a-programme, accessed on 11 October 2017.

DfE (2015a) *Special Educational Needs and Disability (SEN) Code of Practice: 0 to 25 Years*. London: DfE. Available at www.gov.uk/government/publications/send-code-of-practice-0-to-25, accessed on 1 May 2018.

DfE (2015b) *Children with Special Educational Needs: An Analysis – 2015*. London: DfE. Available at www.gov.uk/government/statistics/announcements/children-with-special-educational-needs-an-analysis-2015, accessed on 14 December 2015.

DfE (2015c) *Reading: Supporting Higher Standards in Schools.* London: DfE. Available at www.gov.uk/government/publications/reading-supporting-higher-standards-in-schools, accessed on 3 September 2018.

DfE (2016a) *Phonics Screening Check and Key Stage 1 Assessments: England 2016.* London: DfE. Available at www.gov.uk/government/statistics/phonics-screening-check-and-key-stage-1-assessments-england-2016, accessed on 9 October 2017.

DfE (2016b) *Schools, Pupils and their Characteristics: January 2016.* London: DfE. Available at www.gov.uk/government/statistics/schools-pupils-and-their-characteristics-january-2016, accessed on 20 December 2018.

DfE (2017a) *Schools, Pupils and their Characteristics: January 2017.* London: DfE. Available at www.gov.uk/government/statistics/schools-pupils-and-their-characteristics-january-2017, accessed on 17 September 2017.

DfE (2017b) *Revised GCSE and Equivalent Results in England: 2015 to 2016.* London: DfE. Available at www.gov.uk/government/statistics/revised-gcse-and-equivalent-results-in-england-2015-to-2016, accessed on 12 October 2017.

DfE (2017c) *Permanent and Fixed-period Exclusions in England: 2015 to 2016.* London: DfE. Available at www.gov.uk/government/statistics/permanent-and-fixed-period-exclusions-in-england-2015-to-2016, accessed on 26 June 2018.

DH (Department of Health) (2001) *Valuing People: A New Strategy for Learning Disability for the 21st Century.* Cm 5086. London: DH.

Dillenburger, K., Jordan, J., McKerr, L. and Keenan, M. (2015) 'The Millennium child with autism: Early childhood trajectories for health, education and economic wellbeing.' *Developmental Neurorehabilitation 18*, 1, 37–46.

Dockrell, J. and Shield, B. (2006) 'Acoustical barriers in classrooms: The impact of noise on performance in the classroom.' *British Educational Research Journal 32*, 3, 529–505.

Dockrell, J., Peacey, N. and Lunt, I. (2002) *Literature Review: Meeting the Needs of Children with Special Educational Needs.* London: Institute of Education, University of London.

Dockrell, J., Ricketts, J., Palikara, O., Charman, T. and Lindsay, G. (2012) *Profiles of Need and Provision for Children with Language Impairments and Autism Spectrum Disorders in Mainstream Schools: A Prospective Study.* Research Report DfE-RR247-BCRP9. London: Department for Education.

Douglas, G., Travers, J., McLinden, M., Robertson, C. *et al.* (2012) *Measuring Educational Engagement, Progress and Outcomes for Children with Special Educational Needs: A Review.* Report No. 11. Trim, Ireland: National Council for Special Education.

Downey, R. and Rapport, M.J. (2012) 'Motor activity in children with autism: A review of current literature.' *Pediatric Physical Therapy 24*, 1, 2–20.

Drahota, A., Wood, J., Sze, K. and van Dyke, M. (2010) 'Effects of cognitive behavioural therapy on daily living skills in children with high-functioning autism and concurrent anxiety disorders.' *Journal of Autism Developmental Disorders 41*, 3, 257–265.

Dyson, A. and Farrell, P., with Gallanaugh, F., Hutcheson, G. and Polat, F. (2007) 'But What About the Others? Patterns of Student Achievement in Inclusive Schools.' In R. Cigman (ed.) *Included or Excluded? The Challenge of Mainstream for Some SEN Children* (Chapter 12). Abingdon: Routledge.

Education Act (1981) Available at www.legislation.gov.uk/ukpga/1981/60/contents, accessed on 2 July 2017.

Education Act (1996) Available at www.legislation.gov.uk/ukpga/1996/56/contents, accessed on 5 July 2014.

Education and Inspections Act (2006) Available at www.legislation.gov.uk/ukpga/2006/40/contents, accessed on 14 May 2018.

Education Reform Act (1998) Available at www.legislation.gov.uk/ukpga/1988/40/contents, accessed on 7 March 2019.

Ekblad, L. (2013) 'Autism, personality and human diversity: Defining neurodiversity in an iterative process using Aspie Quiz.' *Sage Open*, July–September, 1–14. doi:10.1177/2158244013497722.

Emam, M. and Farrell, P. (2009) 'Tensions experienced by teachers and their views of support for pupils with autism spectrum disorders in mainstream schools.' *European Journal of Special Educational Needs 24*, 4, 407–422.

Equality Act (2010) Available at www.legislation.gov.uk/ukpga/2010/15/contents, accessed on 9 July 2014.

Erevelles, N. (2002) 'Voices of silence: Foucault, disability and the question of self-determination.' *Studies in Philosophy and Education 21*, 1, 17–35.

Evans, B. (2017) *The Metamorphosis of Autism: A History of Child Development in Britain.* Manchester: Manchester University Press.

Fava, L., Vicari, S., Valeri, G., D'Elia, L., Arima, S. and Strauss, K. (2012) 'Intensive behavioural intervention for school-aged children with autism: Una Breccia nel Muro (UBM) – A comprehensive behavioral model.' *Research in Autism Spectrum Disorders 6*, 4, 1273–1288.

Feldman, E., Kim, J.-S. and Elliott, S. (2011) 'The effects of accommodations on adolescents' self-efficacy and test performance.' *Journal of Special Education 45*, 2, 77–88.

Fentress, G.M. and Lerman, D.C. (2012) 'A comparison of two prompting procedures for teaching basic skills to children with autism.' *Research in Autism Spectrum Disorders 6*, 3, 1083–1090.

Fletcher-Watson, S., Adams, J., Brook, K., Charman, T. *et al.* (2018) 'Making the future together: Shaping autism research through meaningful participation.' *Autism*, 1–11. Available at https://doi.org/10.1177%2F1362361318786721.

Gernsbacher, M.A., Morson, E.M. and Grace, E.J. (2016) 'Language and speech in autism.' *Annual Review of Linguistics 2*, 413–425.

Giles, D. (2013) 'DSM-V is taking away our identity: The reaction of the online community to the proposed changes in the diagnosis of Asperger's disorder.' *Health 18*, 2, 179–195.

Glashan, L., Mackay, G. and Grieve, A. (2004) 'Teachers' experience of support in the mainstream education of pupils with autism.' *Improving Schools 7*, 1, 49–60.

Glidden, D., Bouman, W.P., Jones, B.A. and Arcelus, J. (2016) 'Gender dysphoria and autism spectrum disorder: A systematic review of the literature.' *Sexual Medicine Reviews 4*, 1, 3–14.

Goodall, C. (2018) '"I felt closed in and like I couldn't breathe": A qualitative study exploring the mainstream educational experiences of autistic young people.' *Autism and Developmental Language Impairments 3*, 1–16.

Gould, J. (2017) 'Towards understanding the under-recognition of girls and women on the autism spectrum.' *Autism 21*, 6, 703–705.

Gould, J. and Ashton-Smith, J. (2011) 'Missed diagnosis or misdiagnosis? Girls and women on the autism spectrum.' *Good Autism Practice 12*, 1, 34–41.

Green, J., Absoud, M., Grahame, V., Malik, O. *et al.* (2018) 'Pathological demand avoidance: Symptoms but not a syndrome.' *The Lancet: Child & Adolescent Health 2*, 6, 455–464.

Grinker, R. (2015) 'Reframing the science and anthropology of autism.' *Culture, Medicine and Psychiatry 39*, 2, 345–350.

Grondhuis, S. and Aman, M. (2012) 'Assessment of anxiety in children and adolescents with autism spectrum disorders.' *Research in Autism Spectrum Disorders 6*, 4, 1345–1365.

Grove, R., Hoekstra, R.A., Wierda, M. and Begeer, S. (2018,) 'Special interests and subjective wellbeing in autistic adults.' *Autism Research 11*, 5, 766–775.

Guldberg, K. (2010) 'Educating children on the autism spectrum: Preconditions for inclusion and notions of "best autism practice" in the early years.' *British Journal of Special Education 37*, 4, 168–174.

Gunn, K. and Delafield-Butt, J. (2016) 'Teaching children with autism spectrum disorder with restricted interests: A review of evidence for best practice.' *Review of Educational Research 86*, 2, 408–430.

Hannah, L.A. and Stagg, S.D. (2016) 'Experiences of sex education and sexual awareness in young adults with autism spectrum disorder.' *Journal of Autism and Developmental Disorders 46*, 12, 3678–3687.

Happé, F. (1994) 'Wechsler IQ profile and theory of mind in autism: A research note.' *The Journal of Child Psychiatry and Psychology 35*, 8, 1461–1471.

Happé, F. (2015) 'Are We Really any Closer to Our Understanding of Autism across the Whole Spectrum? Important Headlines from Autism Research.' 'Looking Forward, Looking Back: The Janus View of Autism' Conference. London, 25–26 November 2015.

Happé, F. and Charlton, R.A. (2012) 'Aging in autism spectrum disorders: A mini-review.' *Gerontology 58*, 1, 70–78.

Happé, F. and Frith, U. (2006) 'The weak coherence account: Detail-focused cognitive style in autism spectrum disorders.' *Journal of Autism and Developmental Disorders 36*, 1, 5–25.

Happé F., Ronald, A. and Plomin R. (2006) 'Time to give up on a single explanation for autism.' *Nature Neuroscience 9*, 10, 1218–1220.

Happé, F., Booth, R., Charlton, R. and Hughes, C. (2006) 'Executive function deficits in autism spectrum disorders and attention-deficit/hyperactivity disorder: Examining profiles across domains and ages.' *Brain and Cognition 61*, 1, 25–39.

Harvey, J.A. (2011) 'What's so Special about Special? Improving Inclusion for Children with Autism in Mainstream Schools.' Doctor of Applied Child and Educational Psychology Thesis. Birmingham: University of Birmingham. Available at http://etheses.bham. ac.uk/3287/1/Harvey_12_Applied_Vol1.pdf, accessed on 12 November 2013.

Hearst, C. (2016) 'Voices from the Constellation #17: Caroline Hearst on Neurodiversity and Autism Advocacy.' Learn from Autistics: Connecting Parents and Caregivers with Autistic Voices. Available at http://learnfromautistics.com/voices-constellation-17-caroline-hearst-neurodiversity-autism-advocacy/, accessed on 2 January 2017.

Heasman, B. and Gillespie, A. (2017) 'Perspective-taking is two-sided: Misunderstandings between people with Asperger's syndrome and their family members.' *Autism 22*, 6, 740–750.

Heasman, B. and Gillespie, A. (2018) 'Neurodivergent intersubjectivity: Distinctive features of how autistic people create shared understanding.' *Autism*, 1–12. Available at https://doi.org/10.1177%2F1362361318785172.

Hebron, J. and Humphrey, N. (2013) 'Exposure to bullying among students with autism spectrum conditions: A multi-informant analysis of risk and protective factors.' *Autism 18*, 6, 618–630.

Hehir, T., Grindal, T., Freeman, B., Lamoreau, R., Borquaye, Y. and Burke, S. (2016) *A Summary of the Evidence on Inclusive Education*. São Paulo and Cambridge: Instituto Alana, Abt Associates.

Higashida, N. (2014) *The Reason I Jump: One Boy's Voice from the Silence of Autism*. London: Sceptre.

Higashida, N. (2017) *Fall Down 7 Times, Get Up 8*. London: Sceptre.

Hendrickx, S. (2015) *Women and Girls with Autism Spectrum Disorder: Understanding Life Experiences from Early Childhood to Old Age*. London: Jessica Kingsley Publishers.

Hesmondhalgh, M. (2006) *Autism, Access and Inclusion on the Front Line: Confessions of an Autism Anorak*. London: Jessica Kingsley Publishers.

Hesmondhalgh, M. and Breakey, H. (2001) *Access and Inclusion for Children with Autistic Spectrum Disorders: Let Me In*. London: Jessica Kingsley Publishers.

Hidi, S. and Renninger, A. (2006) 'The four-phase model of interest development.' *Educational Psychologist 41*, 2, 111–127.

Hirvikoski, T., Mittendorfer-Rutz, E., Boman, M. and Larsson, H. (2016) 'Premature mortality in autism spectrum disorder.' *The British Journal of Psychiatry 208*, 3, 232–238.

Hodge, N. and Runswick-Cole, K. (2008) 'Problematising parent–professional partnerships in education.' *Disability & Society 23*, 6, 637–647.

Howlin, P., Mawhood, L. and Rutter, M. (2000) 'Autism and developmental receptive language disorder – A follow-up comparison in early adult life. II: Social, behavioural, and psychiatric outcomes.' *Journal for Child Psychology and Psychiatry 41*, 5, 561–578.

Howlin, P., Moss, P., Savage, S. and Rutter, M. (2013) 'Social outcomes in mid- to later adulthood among individuals diagnosed with autism and average nonverbal IQ as children.' *Journal of the American Academy of Child & Adolescent Psychiatry 52*, 6, 572–581.

Hughes, B. (2009) 'Disability activisms: Social model stalwarts and biological citizens.' *Disability & Society 24*, 6, 677–688.

Hull, L., Petrides, K.V., Allison, C., Smith, P. *et al.* (2017) '"Putting on my best normal": Social camouflaging in adults with autism spectrum conditions.' *Journal of Autism and Developmental Disorders 47*, 8, 2519–2534.

Humphrey, N. (2008) 'Including pupils with autistic spectrum disorders in mainstream schools.' *Support for Learning 23*, 1, 41–47.

Humphrey, N. and Lewis, S. (2008) '"Make me normal": The views and experiences of pupils on the autistic spectrum in mainstream secondary schools.' *Autism 12*, 1, 23–46.

Humphrey, N. and Squires, G. (2011) *Achievement for All: National Evaluation.* DfE Research Report DFE-RR123. London: Department for Education.

Humphrey, N. and Symes, W. (2011) 'Inclusive education for pupils with autistic spectrum disorders in secondary mainstream schools: Teacher attitudes, experience and knowledge.' *International Journal of Inclusive Education 17*, 1, 32–46.

Humphrey, N., Bartolo, P., Ale, P., Calleja, C. *et al.* (2006) 'Understanding and responding to diversity in the primary classroom: An international study.' *European Journal of Teacher Education 29*, 3, 305–318.

Hurst, R. (2000) 'To revise or not to revise?' *Disability & Society 15*, 7, 1083–1087.

Imray, P. and Colley, A. (2017) *Inclusion is Dead: Long Live Inclusion.* Abingdon: Routledge.

Jacobson, J.W., Mulick, J.A. and Schwartz, A.A. (1995) 'A history of facilitated communication: Science, pseudoscience, and antiscience science working group on facilitated communication.' *American Psychologist 50*, 9, 750–765.

Jacques, C., Courchesne, V., Meilleur, A.-A., Mineau, S. *et al.* (2018) 'What interests young autistic children? An exploratory study of object exploration and repetitive behavior.' *PLOS One 13*, 2, 1–17.

Johnston, P. (1985) 'Understanding reading disability: A case study approach.' *Harvard Educational Review 55*, 2, 153–177.

Jones, G. (2002) *Educational Provision for Children with Autism and Asperger Syndrome: Meeting their Needs.* London: David Fulton Publishers.

Jones, G., Baker, L., English, A. and Lyn-Cook, L. (2011) *National Autism Standards.* London: Autism Education Trust.

Jones, G., English, A., Guldberg, K., Jordan, R., Richardson, P. and Waltz, M. (2008) *Educational Provision for Children and Young People on the Autism Spectrum Living in England: A Review of Current Practice, Issues and Challenges.* London: Autism Education Trust.

Jordan, R. (2005) 'Autistic Spectrum Disorders.' In A. Lewis and B. Norwich (eds) *Special Teaching for Special Children? Pedagogies for Inclusion* (pp.110–122). Maidenhead: Open University Press.

Kapp, S., Gillespie-Lynch, K., Sherman, L. and Hutman, T. (2013) 'Deficit, difference, or both? Autism and neurodiversity.' *Developmental Psychology 49*, 1, 59–71.

Kelly-Gadol, J. (1987) 'The Social Relation of the Sexes: Methodological Implications of Women's History.' In S. Harding (ed.) *Feminism and Methodology* (pp.15–28). Bloomington, IN: Indiana University Press.

Kenny, L., Hattersley, C., Molins, B., Buckley, C., Povey, C. and Pellicano, E. (2016) 'Which terms should be used to describe autism? Perspectives from the UK autism community.' *Autism 20*, 4, 442–462.

Kim, H. (2012) 'Autism across cultures: Rethinking autism.' *Disability & Society 27*, 4, 535–545.

Kim, Y.S., Leventhal, B., Koh, Y., Fombonne, E. *et al.* (2011) 'Prevalence of autism spectrum disorders in a total population sample.' *American Journal of Psychiatry 168*, 9, 904–912.

Kispal, A. (2008) *Effective Teaching of Inference Skills for Reading.* National Foundation for Educational Research, Research Report DCSF-RR031. London: Department for Children, Schools and Families.

Klar-Wolfond, E. (2008) 'The Mismeasure of Autism: The Basis for Current Autism "Advocacy".' In W. Lawson (ed.) *Concepts of Normality: The Autistic and Typical Spectrum* (pp.104–129). London: Jessica Kingsley Publishers.

Klatte, M., Bergström, K. and Lachmann, T. (2013) 'Does noise affect learning? A short review on noise effects on cognitive performance in children.' *Frontiers in Psychology 4*, article 578, 1–6.

Knüppel, A., Telléus, G.K. and Lauritsen, M.B. (2018) 'Description of a Danish nationwide survey of adolescents and adults diagnosed with autism spectrum disorders in childhood: The AutCome Study.' *Journal of Mental Health Research in Intellectual Disabilities 11*, 4, 266–286.

Koenig, K.P. and Williams, L.H. (2017) 'Characterization and utilization of preferred interests: A survey of adults on the autism spectrum.' *Occupational Therapy in Mental Health 33*, 2, 129–140.

Kourti, M. and MacLeod, A. (2018) '"I don't feel like a gender, I feel like myself": Autistic individuals raised as girls exploring gender identity.' *Autism in Adulthood 1*, 1, 1–8.

Kovshoff, H., Hastings, R.P. and Remington, B. (2011) 'Two-year outcomes for children with autism after the cessation of early intensive behavioral intervention.' *Behavior Modification 35*, 5, 427–450.

Kushki, A., Chau, T. and Anagnostou, E. (2011) 'Handwriting difficulties in children with autism spectrum disorders: A scoping review.' *Journal of Autism and Developmental Disorders 41*, 12, 1706–1716.

Laugeson, E.A., Frankel, F., Gantman, A., Dillon, A.R. and Mogi, C. (2012) 'Evidence-based social skills training for adolescents with autism spectrum disorders: The UCLA PEERS Program.' *Journal of Autism and Developmental Disorders 42*, 6, 1025–1036.

Lawson, W. (2008) *Concepts of Normality (The Autistic and Typical Spectrum)*. London: Jessica Kingsley Publishers.

Lawson, W. (2011) *The Passionate Mind: How People with Autism Learn*. London: Jessica Kingsley Publishers.

Lawson, W. (2014). 'Autism Spectrum Conditions (ASC), Ethics and Issues of Gender.' 'Autism and Ethics' Conference. Inverness, 16 May 2014. Autism Rights Group Highland and National Autistic Society Scotland. Available at www.arghighland. co.uk/ethics.html

Lawson, W. (2015) 'Gender dysphoria and autism.' Network Autism. 26 May. Available at https://network.autism.org.uk/knowledge/insight-opinion/gender-dysphoria-and-autism

Lazarus, S., Thurlow, M., Lail, K. and Christensen, L. (2009) 'A longitudinal analysis of state accommodations policies: Twelve years of change, 1993–2005.' *The Journal of Special Education 43*, 2, 67–80.

Lee, A., Hobson, R.P. and Chiat, S.J. (1994) 'I, you, me, and autism: An experimental study.' *Journal of Developmental Disorders 24*, 2, 155–176.

Lenehan, C. (2017) *These Are Our Children*. London: Council for Disabled Children.

Lewis, A. (2010) 'Silence in the context of "child voice".' *Children & Society 24*, 1, 14–23.

Lewis, A. and Norwich, B. (eds) (2005) *Special Teaching for Special Children? Pedagogies for Inclusion*. Maidenhead: Open University Press.

Liasidou, A. (2012) *Inclusive Education, Politics and Policymaking*. London: Continuum International Publishing Group.

Lindsay, G. (2007) 'Educational psychology and the effectiveness of inclusive education/ mainstreaming.' *British Journal of Educational Psychology 77*, 1, 1–24.

Linton, K., Taylor, E., Sensui, L. and Spillers, J. (2013) 'Opinions of people who self-identify with autism and Asperger's on DSM-5 criteria.' *Research on Social Work Practice 24*, 1, 67–77.

Lloyd-Smith, M. and Tarr, J. (2000) 'A Sociological Dimension.' In A. Lewis and G. Lindsay (eds) *Researching Children's Perspectives* (pp.59–70). Buckingham: Open University Press.

Locke, J., Ishijima, E.H., Kasari, C. and London, N. (2010) 'Loneliness, friendship quality and the social networks of adolescents with high-functioning autism in an inclusive school setting.' *Journal of Research in Special Educational Needs 10*, 2, 74–81.

Loveland, K., McEvoy, R., Tunali, B. and Kelley, M. (1990) 'Narrative story telling in autism and Down's Syndrome.' *British Journal of Developmental Psychology 8*, 1, 9–23.

Lundström, S., Reichenberg, A., Melke, J., Råstam, M. *et al.* (2015) 'Autism spectrum disorders and coexisting disorders in a nationwide Swedish twin study.' *The Journal of Child Psychology and Psychiatry 56*, 6, 702–710.

Matson, J., Turygin, N., Beighley, J., Rieske, R. *et al.* (2012) 'Applied behaviour analysis in autism spectrum disorders: Recent developments, strengths and pitfalls', *Research in Autism Spectrum Disorders 6*, 1, 144–150.

Mawhood, L., Howlin, P. and Rutter, M. (2000) 'Autism and developmental receptive language disorder – A comparative follow-up in early adult life. 1: Cognitive and language outcomes.' *Journal for Child Psychology and Psychiatry 41*, 5, 547–559.

McAllister, K. and Sloan, S. (2016) 'Designed by the pupils, for the pupils: An autism-friendly school.' *British Journal of Special Education 43*, 4, 330–357.

McConnell, S. (2002) 'Interventions to facilitate social interaction for young children with autism: Review of available research and recommendations for educational intervention and future research.' *Journal of Autism and Developmental Disorders 32*, 5, 351–372.

McDonnell, A. and Milton, D. (2014) 'Going with the flow: Reconsidering "repetitive behaviour" through the concept of "flow states".' In G. Jones and E. Hurley (eds) *Good Autism Practice: Autism, Happiness and Wellbeing* (pp.38–47). Birmingham: BILD.

McKenna, A., Stevenson, K., Timmins, S. and Bindman, M. (2017) 'Developing an autism spectrum disorder assessment pathway for children presenting with selective mutism.' *Archives of Disease in Childhood 2017 102*, Suppl. 3, A1–A31.

McNaughton, D. and Light, L. (2013) 'The iPad and mobile technology revolution: Benefits and challenges for individuals who require augmentative and alternative communication.' *Augmentative and Alternative Communication 29*, 2, 107–116.

Mehrabian, A. and Ferris, S.R. (1967) 'Inference of attitudes from nonverbal communication in two channels.' *Journal of Consulting Psychology 31*, 248–252.

Menzinger, B. and Jackson, R. (2009) 'The effect of light intensity and noise on the classroom behaviour of pupils with Asperger Syndrome.' *Support for Learning 24*, 4, 170–175.

Mercati, O., Huguet, G., Danckaert, A., André-Leroux, G. *et al.* (2017) 'CNTN6 mutations are risk factors for abnormal auditory sensory perception in autism spectrum disorders.' *Molecular Psychiatry 22*, 4, 625–633.

Merwin, R.M., Moskovich, A.A., Wagner, H.R., Ritschel, L.A., Craighead, L.W. and Zucker, N.L. (2013) 'Emotion regulation difficulties in anorexia nervosa: Relationship to self-perceived sensory sensitivity.' *Cognition and Emotion 27*, 3, 441–452.

Mesibov, G. (1984) 'Social skills training with verbal autistic adolescents and adults: A program model.' *Journal of Autism and Developmental Disorders 14*, 4, 395–404.

Mesibov, G. and Howley, M. (2003) *Accessing the Curriculum for Pupils with Autistic Spectrum Disorders: Using the TEACCH Programme to Help Inclusion.* London: David Fulton Publishers Limited.

Michael, C. (2016) 'Why we need research about autism and ageing.' *Autism 20*, 5, 515–516.

Millar, R., McCann, J., Scott, L., Doherty, K. *et al.* (2002) *Autistic Spectrum Disorders: A Guide to Classroom Practice.* Dublin: Department of Education.

Milton, D. (2012a) 'The ontological status of autism: The "double empathy problem".' *Disability & Society 27*, 6, 883–887.

Milton, D. (2012b) 'So what exactly is autism?' *AET Professional Competency Framework.* Available at www.autismeducationtrust.org.uk, accessed on 3 March 2014.

Milton, D. (2014a) 'So what exactly are autism interventions intervening with?' *Good Autism Practice 15*, 2, 6–14.

Milton, D. (2014b) 'Autistic expertise: A critical reflection on the production of knowledge in autism studies.' *Autism 18*, 7, 794–802.

Milton, D. and Sims, T. (2016) 'How is a sense of well-being and belonging constructed in the accounts of autistic adults?' *Disability & Society 31*, 4, 520–534.

Miniscalco, C., Hagberg, B., Kadesjö, B., Westerlund, M. and Gillberg, C. (2007) 'Narrative skills, cognitive profiles and neuropsychiatric disorders in 7–8-year-old children with late developing language.' *International Journal of Language & Communication Disorders* 42, 6, 665–681.

Mitchell, S., Brian, J., Zwaigenbaum, L., Roberts, W. *et al.* (2006) 'Early language and communication development of infants later diagnosed with Autism Spectrum Disorder.' *Journal of Developmental and Behavioral Pediatrics* 27, 2, 69–78.

Molloy, H. and Vasil, L. (2002) 'The social construction of Asperger syndrome: The pathologising of difference.' *Disability & Society* 17, 6, 659–669.

Mooneyham, B. and Schooler, J. (2013) 'The costs and benefits of mind-wandering: A review.' *Canadian Journal of Experimental Psychology* 67, 1, 11–18.

Mottron, L., Bouvet, L., Bonnel, A., Samson, F. *et al.* (2013) 'Vertical mapping in the development of exceptional autistic abilities.' *Neuroscience and Behavioral Reviews* 37, 2, 209–228.

Moudon, A. (2009) 'Real noise from the urban environment: How ambient community noise affects health and what can be done about it.' *American Journal of Preventive Medicine* 37, 2, 167–171.

Moyse, R. and Porter, J. (2014) 'The experience of the hidden curriculum for autistic girls at mainstream primary schools.' *European Journal of Special Needs Education* 30, 2, 187–201.

Murray, D. (2014) 'Participation and Scope.' 'Participation and Inclusion from the Inside Out: Seeing Autism from an Autistic Perspective' Conference. London: National Autistic Society, 28 April 2014.

Murray, D. and Lawson, W. (2007) 'Inclusion through Technology for Autistic Children.' In R. Cigman (ed.) *Included or Excluded? The Challenge of the Mainstream for Some SEN Children* (pp.151–158). Abingdon: Routledge.

Murray, D., Lesser, M. and Lawson, W. (2005) 'Attention, monotropism and the diagnostic criteria for autism.' *Autism* 9, 2, 136–156.

Muskett, T. (2016) 'Examining Language and Communication in Autism Spectrum Disorder – In Context.' In K. Runswick-Cole, R. Mallett and S. Timimi (eds) *Re-Thinking Autism: Diagnosis, Identity and Equality* (pp.300–316). London: Jessica Kingsley Publishers.

Nation, K., Clarke, P., Wright, B. and Williams, C. (2006) 'Patterns of reading ability in children with autism spectrum disorder.' *Journal of Autism and Developmental Disorders* 2006, 36, 911–919.

National Academy of Sciences (2015) 'Prevalence of Intellectual Disabilities.' In *Mental Disorders and Disabilities in Low-Income Children*. Washington, DC: National Academies Press.

National Literacy Trust (2017) 'What is Phonics?' Available at https://literacytrust.org.uk/information/what-is-literacy/what-phonics/, accessed on 9 October 2017.

Nolan, J. and McBride (2015) 'Embodied Semiosis: Autistic "Stimming" as Sensory Praxis.' In P. Trifonas (ed.) *International Handbook of Semiotics, vol. 1* (pp.1069–1078). Dordrecht: Springer.

Norbury, C.F. and Bishop, D.V.M. (2003) 'Narrative skills of children with communication impairments.' *International Journal of Language and Communication Disorders* 38, 3, 287–313.

Norbury, C.F. and Nation, K. (2011) 'Understanding variability in reading comprehension in adolescents with autism spectrum disorders: Interactions with language status and decoding skill.' *Scientific Studies of Reading* 15, 3, 191–210.

Norbury, C.F., Griffiths, H. and Nation, K. (2010) 'Sound before meaning: Word learning in autistic disorders.' *Neuropsychologia* 48, 14, 4012–4019.

Norwich, B. (2008) *Dilemmas of Difference, Inclusion and Disability: International Perspectives and Future Directions*. Abingdon: Routledge.

Norwich, B. (2014) 'Government Policy and Where Pupils with SEN/Disabilities go to School.' BERA (British Educational Research Association) Respecting Children and Young People: Learning from the Past, Redesigning the Future. Available at http://berarespectingchildren.wordpress.com/2014/07/11/government-policy-and-where-pupils-with-sen-disabilities-go-to-school/#more-257, accessed on 14 July 2014.

Norwich, B. and Kelly, N. (2004) 'Pupils' views on inclusion: Moderate learning difficulties and bullying in mainstream and special schools.' British Educational Research Journal 30, 1, 43–65.

Norwich, B. and Lewis, A. (2007) 'How specialized is teaching children with disabilities and difficulties?' Journal of Curriculum Studies 39, 2, 127–150.

Office of the Children's Commissioner (2012) '"They never give up on you": Schools' Exclusions Inquiry.' London: Office of the Children's Commissioner.

Office of the Children's Commissioner (2017) Briefing: Falling through the Gaps in Education. London: Office of the Children's Commissioner.

ONS (Office for National Statistics) (2011) 2011 Census. Available at www.ons.gov.uk/census/2011census, accessed on 17 July 2013.

Owens, G., Granader, Y., Humphrey, A. and Baron-Cohen, S. (2008) 'LEGO® therapy and the Social Use of Language Programme: An evaluation of two social skills interventions for children with high functioning autism and Asperger Syndrome.' Journal of Autism and Developmental Disorders 38, 1944–1957.

Papadopoulous, C. (2016) 'Stigma towards individuals diagnosed with autistic spectrum disorder: A comparison of UK-based Nigerians and English attitudes.' XI Autism-Europe International Congress 2016. Edinburgh, 16–18 September 2016.

Parsons, S., Guldberg, K., Macleod, A., Jones, G., Prunty, A. and Balfe, T. (2011) 'International review of the evidence on best practice in educational provision for children on the autism spectrum.' European Journal of Special Educational Needs 26, 1, 47–63.

Pellicano, E., Dinsmore, A. and Charman, T. (2013) A Future Made Together: Shaping Autism Research in the UK. London: Institute of Education.

Pellicano, E., Hill, V., Croydon, A., Greathead, S., Kenny, L. and Yates, R. (2014) My Life at School: Understanding the Experiences of Children and Young People with Special Educational Needs in Residential Special Schools. London: Institute of Education.

Pfeiffer, D. (2000) 'The devils are in the details: The ICIDH2 and the disability movement.' Disability & Society 15, 7, 1079–1082.

Pickles, A., le Couteur, A., Leadbitter, K., Salomone, E. et al. (2016) 'Parent-mediated social communication therapy for young children with autism (PACT): Long-term follow-up of a randomised controlled trial.' The Lancet 388, 10059, 2501–2509.

Pilorge, M., Fassier, C., le Corronc, H., Potey, A. et al. (2016) 'Genetic and functional analyses demonstrate a role for abnormal glycinergic signaling in autism.' Molecular Psychiatry 21, 7, 936–945.

Preece, D. and Howley, M. (2018) 'An approach to supporting young people with autism spectrum disorder and high anxiety to re-engage with formal education – The impact on young people and their families.' International Journal of Adolescence and Youth 23, 4, 468–481.

Rajendran, G. and Mitchell, P. (2007) 'Cognitive theories of autism.' Developmental Review 27, 2, 224–260.

Rao, P.A., Beidel, D.C. and Murray, M.J. (2008) 'Social skills interventions for children with Asperger's syndrome or high-functioning autism: A review and recommendations.' Journal of Autism and Developmental Disorders 38, 2, 353–361.

Rapin, I. and Dunn, M. (2003) 'Update on the language disorders of individuals on the autism spectrum.' Brain and Development 25, 3, 166–172.

Ravet, J. (2011) 'Inclusive/exclusive? Contradictory perspectives on autism and inclusion: The case for an integrative position.' International Journal of Inclusive Education 15, 6, 667–682.

Remington, A., Hanley, M., O'Brien, S., Riby, D.M. and Swettenham, J. (2019) 'Implications of capacity in the classroom: Simplifying tasks for autistic children may not be the answer.' Research in Developmental Disabilities 85, 2019, 197–204.

Remington, B., Hastings, R., Kovshoff, H., degli Espinosa, F. *et al.* (2007) 'Early intensive behavioral intervention: Outcomes for children with autism and their parents after two years.' *American Journal of Mental Retardation 112*, 6, 418–438.

Ricketts, J., Jones, C.R.G., Happé, F. and Charman, T. (2013) 'Reading comprehension in autism spectrum disorders: The role of oral language and social functioning.' *Journal of Autism and Developmental Disorders 43*, 4, 807–816.

Rioux, M. and Valentine, F. (2006) 'Does Theory Matter? Exploring the Nexus between Disability, Human Rights and Public Policy.' In D. Pothier and R. Devlin (eds) *Critical Disability Theory: Essays in Philosophy, Politics, Policy and Law* (pp.47–69). Vancouver, BC: UBC Press.

Robertson, K., Chamberlain, B. and Kasari, C. (2003) 'General education teachers' relationships with included students with autism.' *Journal of Autism and Developmental Disorders 33*, 2, 123–130.

Robins, D., Fein, D., Barton, M. and Green, J. (2001) 'The modified checklist for autism in toddlers: An initial study investigating the early detection of autism and pervasive developmental disorders.' *Journal of Autism and Developmental Disorders 31*, 2, 131–144.

Rosenthal, M., Wallace, G.L., Lawson, R., Wills, M.C. *et al.* (2013) 'Impairments in real-world executive function increase from childhood to adolescence in autism spectrum disorders.' *Neuropsychology 27*, 1, 13–18.

Roulstone, S., Wren, Y., Bakopoulou, I., Goodlad, S. and Lindsay, G. (2012) *Exploring Interventions for Children and Young People with Speech, Language and Communication Needs: A Study of Practice.* Research Report DFE-RR247-BCRP13. London: Department for Education.

Runswick-Cole, K. and Hodge, N. (2009) 'Needs or rights? A challenge to the discourse of special education.' *British Journal of Special Education 36*, 4, 198–203.

Runswick-Cole, K., Mallett, R. and Timimi, S. (eds) (2016) *Re-Thinking Autism: Diagnosis, Identity and Equality.* London: Jessica Kingsley Publishers.

Sainsbury, C. (2009) *Martian in the Playground: Understanding the Schoolchild with Asperger's Syndrome.* London: Sage Publications.

Sano, A. and Picard, R.W. (2013) 'Stress Recognition using Wearable Sensors and Mobile Phones.' Humaine Association Conference on 'Affective Computing and Intelligent Interaction', Geneva: IEEE Computer Society, September. doi:10.1109/ACII.2013.117.

Schlosser, R., Balandin, S., Hemsley, B., Iacono, T., Probst, P. and von Tetzchner, S. (2014) 'Facilitated communication and authorship: A systematic review.' *Augmentative and Alternative Communication 30*, 4, 359–358.

Secret Teacher, The (2016) 'We end up hindering the pupils we're meant to help.' *The Guardian*, 12 November.

Segers, M. and Rawana, J. (2014) 'What do we know about suicidality in autism spectrum disorders? A systematic review.' *Autism Research 7*, 4, 507–521.

Shah, P., Hall, R., Catmur, C. and Bird, G. (2016) 'Alexithymia, not autism, is associated with impaired interoception.' *Cortex 81*, 215–220.

Shakespeare, T. (2014) *Disability Rights and Wrongs Revisited*, 2nd edn. Abingdon: Routledge.

Sharples, J., Webster, R. and Blatchford, P. (2015) *Making Best Use of Teaching Assistants: Guidance Report.* London: Education Endowment Foundation.

Shield, B. and Dockrell, J. (2004) 'External and internal noise surveys of London primary schools.' *The Journal of the Acoustical Society of America 115*, 2, 730–738.

Siegel, L. (1989) 'IQ is irrelevant to the definition of learning disabilities.' *Journal of Learning Disabilities 22*, 8, 469–478.

Sinclair, J. (1999) 'Why I dislike "person first" language.' Autism Mythbusters. Available at http://autismmythbusters.com/general-public/autistic-vs-people-with-autism/jim-sinclair-why-i-dislike-person-first-language/, accessed on 14 June 2013.

Sinclair Taylor, A. (1995) '"Less Better Than The Rest": Perceptions of integration in a multi-ethnic special needs unit.' *Educational Review 47*, 3, 263–274.

Sinclair Taylor, A. (2000) 'The UN Convention and the Rights of the Child: Giving Children a Voice.' In A. Lewis and G. Lindsay (eds) *Researching Children's Perspectives* (pp.21–33). Buckingham: Open University Press.

Singer, J. (1998) 'Odd People In: The Birth of Community amongst People on the Autism Spectrum: A Personal Exploration of a New Social Movement based on Neurological Diversity.' Honours thesis presented to the Faculty of Humanities and Social Science, University of Technology, Sydney, Australia.

Singh, A., Uijtdewilligen, L., Twisk, J., van Mechelen, W. and Chinapaw, M. (2012) 'Physical activity and performance at school: A systematic review of the literature including a methodological quality assessment.' *Archives of Pediatrics and Adolescent Medicine 166,* 1, 49–55.

Slee, R. and Allan, J. (2001) 'Excluding the included: A reconsideration of inclusive education.' *International Studies in Sociology of Education 11,* 2, 173–192.

Special Educational Needs and Disability Act (2001) Available at www.legislation.gov.uk/ ukpga/2001/10/contents, accessed on 7 March 2019.

Sproston, K., Sedgewick, F. and Crane, L. (2017) 'Autistic girls and school exclusion: Perspectives of students and their parents.' *Autism & Developmental Language Impairments 2,* 1–14.

STA (Standards and Testing Agency) (2017) *2018 Access Arrangements Guidance.* Report STA/18/8115/e. London: Department for Education.

Stewart, C. (2016) 'Cygnets to swans – Supporting girls on the spectrum in the education setting from primary school onwards.' 'From Exclusion to Inclusion: How to Transform Autism Education' Conference. Transform Autism Education Project. Birmingham, 13 October 2016.

Sweileh, W., Al-Jabi, S., Sawalha, A. and Zyoud, S. (2016) 'Bibliometric profile of the global scientific research on autism spectrum disorders.' *SpringerPlus 5,* 1480, 1–12.

Tager-Flusberg, H., Rhea, P. and Lord, C. (2005) 'Language and Communication in Autism.' In F. Volkmar, P. Rhea, I. Klin and D. Cohen (eds) *Handbook of Autism and Pervasive Developmental Disorders, vol. 1,* 3rd edn (pp.335–364). Hoboken, NJ: John Wiley & Sons, Inc.

Tammet, D. (2006) *Born on a Blue Day.* London: Hodder & Stoughton Ltd.

Tarr, M., Tsokova, D. and Takkunen, U.-M. (2012) 'Insights into inclusive education through a small Finnish case study of an inclusive school context.' *International Journal of Inclusive Education 16,* 7, 691–704.

Taylor, B., Jick, H. and MacLaughlin, D. (2013) 'Prevalence and incidence rates of autism in the UK: Time trend from 2004–2010 in children aged 8 years.' *BMJ Open 2013,* 3. doi:10.1136/bmjopen-2013003219.

Terzi, L. (2005) 'Beyond the dilemma of difference: The capability approach to disability and special needs education.' *Journal of Philosophy of Education 39,* 3, 443–459.

Thibault, R. (2014) 'Can autistics redefine autism? The cultural politics of autistic activism.' *Trans-Scripts 4.* Available at www.academia.edu/7234120/Can_Autistics_Redefine_ Autism_The_Cultural_Politics_of_Autistic_Activism, accessed on 13 October 2015.

Thomas, G. (2012) 'A review of thinking and research about inclusive education policy, with suggestions for a new kind of inclusive thinking.' *British Educational Research Journal 39,* 3, 473–490.

Thomas, G. and O'Hanlon, C. (2005) 'Series Editors' Preface.' In A. Lewis and B. Norwich (eds) *Special Teaching for Special Children? Pedagogies for Inclusion* (pp.xi–xii). Maidenhead: Open University Press.

Trudeau, F. and Shephard, R.J. (2008) 'Physical education, school physical activity, school sports and academic performance.' *International Journal of Behavioral Nutrition and Physical Activity 5,* 10. Available at https://doi.org/10.1186/1479-5868-5-10.

UN (United Nations) Committee on the Rights of Persons with Disabilities (2017) *Concluding Observations on the Initial Report of the United Kingdom of Great Britain and Northern Ireland.* CRPD/C/GBR/CO/1. Geneva: UN.

UN DESA (United Nations Department of Economic and Social Affairs) (2006) *Convention on the Rights of Persons with Disabilities (CRPD).* New York: UN. Available at www. un.org/disabilities/convention/conventionfull.shtml, accessed on 15 July 2014.

UNESCO (United Nations Educational, Scientific and Cultural Organization) (1994) *The Salamanca Statement and Framework for Action on Special Needs Education.* Madrid: Ministry of Education and Science.

UNICEF (1989) *United Nations Convention on the Rights of the Child (UNCRC).* London: UNICEF UK.

Vivanti, G., Barbaro, J., Hudry, K., Dissanayake, C. and Prior, M. (2013) 'Intellectual development in autism spectrum disorders: New insights from longitudinal studies.' *Frontiers in Human Neuroscience 7,* 354. doi:10.3389/fnhum.2013.00354.

Walsh, R.J., Krabbendam, L., Dewinter, J. and Begeer, S. (2018) 'Brief report: Gender identity differences in autistic adults: Associations with perceptual and socio-cognitive profiles.' *Journal of Autism and Developmental Disorders 48,* 12, 4070–4078.

Whitaker, P. (2007) 'Provision for youngsters with autistic spectrum disorders in mainstream schools: What parents say – And what parents want.' *British Journal of Special Education 34,* 3, 170–178.

White, R.C. and Remington, A. (2018) 'Object personification in autism: This paper will be very sad if you don't read it.' *Autism.* doi.org/10.1177%2F1362361318793408.

White, S.W. and Roberson-Nay, R. (2009) 'Anxiety, social deficits, and loneliness in youth with autism spectrum disorders.' *Journal of Autism and Developmental Disorders 39,* 7, 1006–1013.

Williams, D. (1992/1999) *Nobody Nowhere,* revised edn. London: Jessica Kingsley Publishers.

Williams, D. (1998) *Autism and Sensing: The Unlost Instinct.* London: Jessica Kingsley Publishers.

Williams, J. and Mavin, S. (2012) 'Disability as constructed difference: A literature review and research agenda for management and organization studies.' *International Journal of Management Reviews 14,* 2, 159–179.

Wing, L. (1980) 'Childhood autism and social class: A question of selection?' *The British Journal of Psychiatry 137,* 5, 410–417.

Wing, L. (2007) 'Children with Autistic Spectrum Disorders.' In R. Cigman (ed.) *Included or Excluded? The Challenge of the Mainstream for Some SEN Children* (pp.23–33). Abingdon: Routledge.

Wing, L. and Gould (1979) 'Severe impairments of social-interaction and associated abnormalities in children: Epidemiology and classification.' *Journal of Autism and Developmental Disorders 9,* 1, 11–29.

Winter-Messiers, M. (2007) 'From tarantulas to toilet brushes: Understanding the special interest areas of children and youth with Asperger syndrome.' *Remedial and Special Education 28,* 3, 140–152.

Wittemeyer, K., English, A., Jones, G., Lyn-Cook, L. and Milton, D. (2011a) *AET Professional Competency Framework.* London: Autism Education Trust.

Wittemeyer, K., Charman, T., Cusack, J., Guldberg, K. *et al.* (2011b) *Educational Provision and Outcomes for People on the Autism Spectrum.* London: Autism Education Trust.

Wood, R. (2016) 'How do autistic children access tests in mainstream primary schools?' *Network Autism.* Available at https://network.autism.org.uk/knowledge/insight-opinion/how-do-autistic-children-access-tests-mainstream-primary-schools, accessed on 20 September 2016.

Wood, R. (2017) 'Testing times – What it's like to sit an exam as an autistic child.' *The Conversation.* Available at https://theconversation.com/testing-times-what-its-like-to-sit-an-exam-as-an-autistic-child-75362, accessed on 30 March 2017.

Wood, R. (2018a) 'The wrong kind of noise: Understanding and valuing the communication of autistic children in schools.' *Educational Review.* Available at https://doi.org/10.1080/00131911.2018.1483895.

Wood, R. (2018b) 'How to help autistic children to socialise in school.' *The Conversation.* Available at https://theconversation.com/how-to-help-autistic-children-socialise-in-school-93616, accessed on 29 March 2017.

Wood, R. (2019) 'Autism, intense interests and support in school: From wasted efforts to shared understandings.' *Educational Review.* Available at https://doi.org/10.1080/001 31911.2019.1566213.

Wood, R. and Milton, D. (2018) 'Reflections on the value of autistic participation in a tri-national teacher-training project through discourses of acceptance, othering and power.' *British Journal of Special Education 45*, 2, 157–171.

Woods, R. (2017) 'Pathological demand avoidance: My thoughts on looping effects and commodification of autism.' *Disability & Society 34*, 5, 753–758.

Woolfenden, S., Sarkozy, V., Ridley, G., Coory, M. and Williams, K. (2012) 'A systematic review of two outcomes in autism spectrum disorder – Epilepsy and mortality.' *Developmental Medicine & Child Neurology 54*, 4, 306–312.

Woolner, P. and Hall, E. (2010) 'Noise in schools: A holistic approach to the issue.' *International Journal of Environmental Research and Public Health 7*, 8, 3255–3269.

World Health Organization (WHO) (2018) ICD-11 (*International Classification of Diseases*, 11th Revision) '6A02 Autism spectrum disorder.' Geneva: WHO. Available at https://icd.who.int/browse11/l-m/en#/http://id.who.int/icd/entity/437815624, accessed on 29 June 2018.

Woronko, D. and Killoran, I. (2011) 'Creating Inclusive Environments for Children with Autism.' In T. Williams (ed.) *Autism Spectrum Disorders – From Genes to Environment.* InTech. doi:10.5772/21136. Available at www.intechopen.com/books/howtoreference/autism-spectrum-disorders-from-genes-to-environment/creating-inclusive-environments-for-children-with-autism, accessed on 3 July 2013.

Zhou, V., Munson, J.A., Greenson, J., Hou, Y., Rogers, S. and Estes, A.M. (2017) 'An exploratory longitudinal study of social and language outcomes in children with autism in bilingual home environments.' *Autism.* Available at https://doi.org/10.1177%2F1362361317743251.

Index